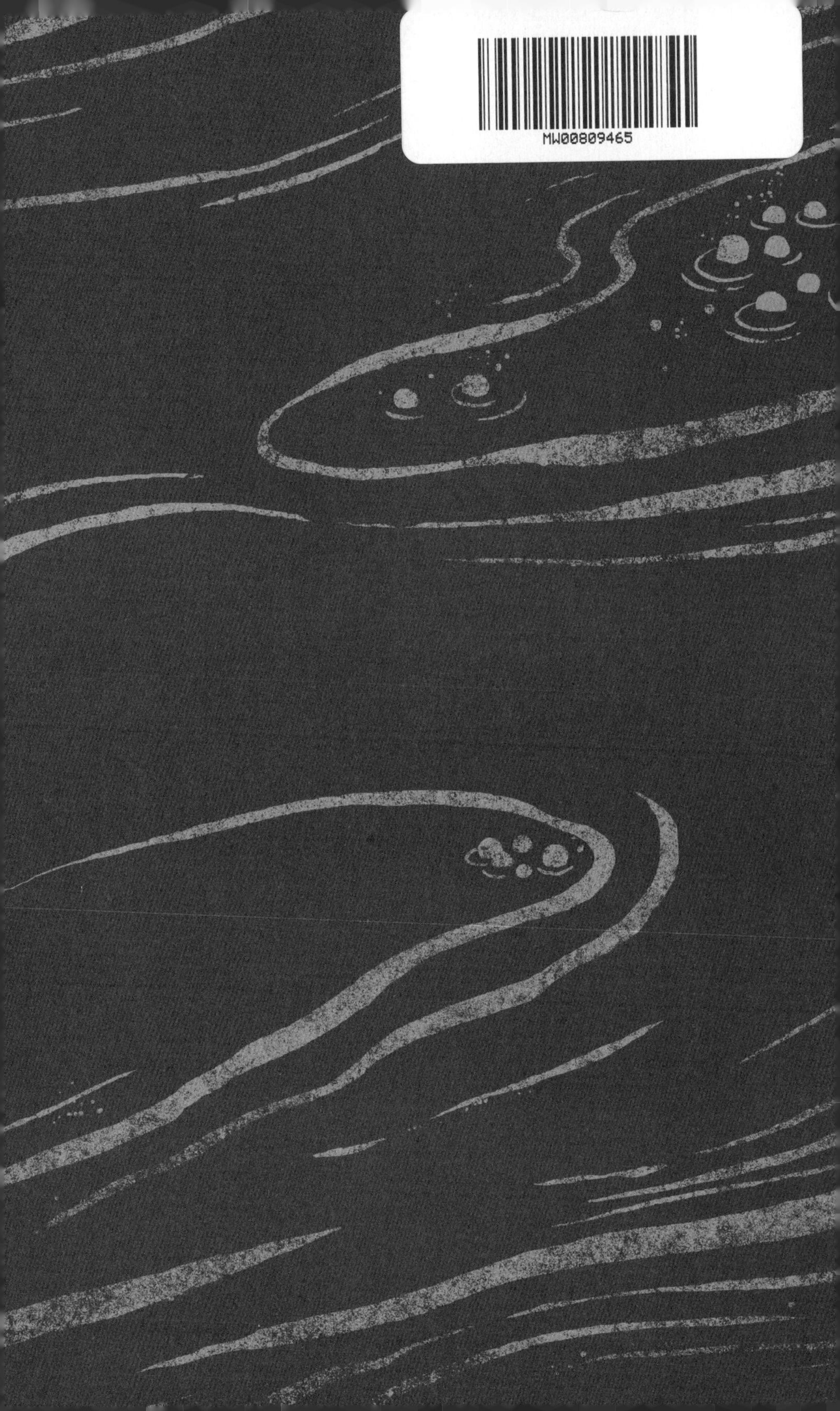

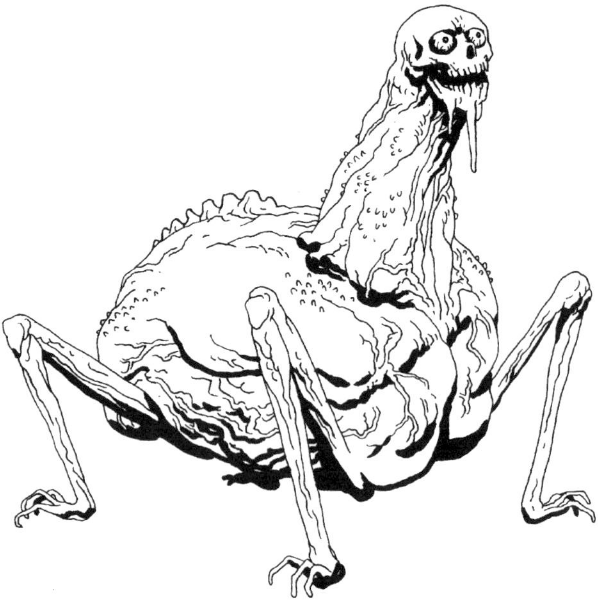

SHIT AND PISS wouldn't have been possible without the love, support, input/influence/interference of the following humans and human-run organizations :

D'anyil Landry, Karyn Morrison, Ramon Sierra, Frank Santoro, Cameron Nicholson, Kate Harmon, Comics Workbook, The Charlottetown Comics Club, Lightning Bolt Comics, The Beguiling, The Copacetic Comics Company, Seite Books, Wooden Bird Comics, Box Brown/Retrofit/Big Planet, and people who are fans of sick shit.

Retrofit 62

Published by Retrofit Comics & Big Planet Comics
Philadelphia • Washington, DC
retrofitcomics.com/bigplanetcomics.com

SHIT AND PISS chapters 1 + 2 previously printed as single issues by Clavicle Cocoris.

Printed in Canada

SHIT AND PISS

TYLER LANDRY

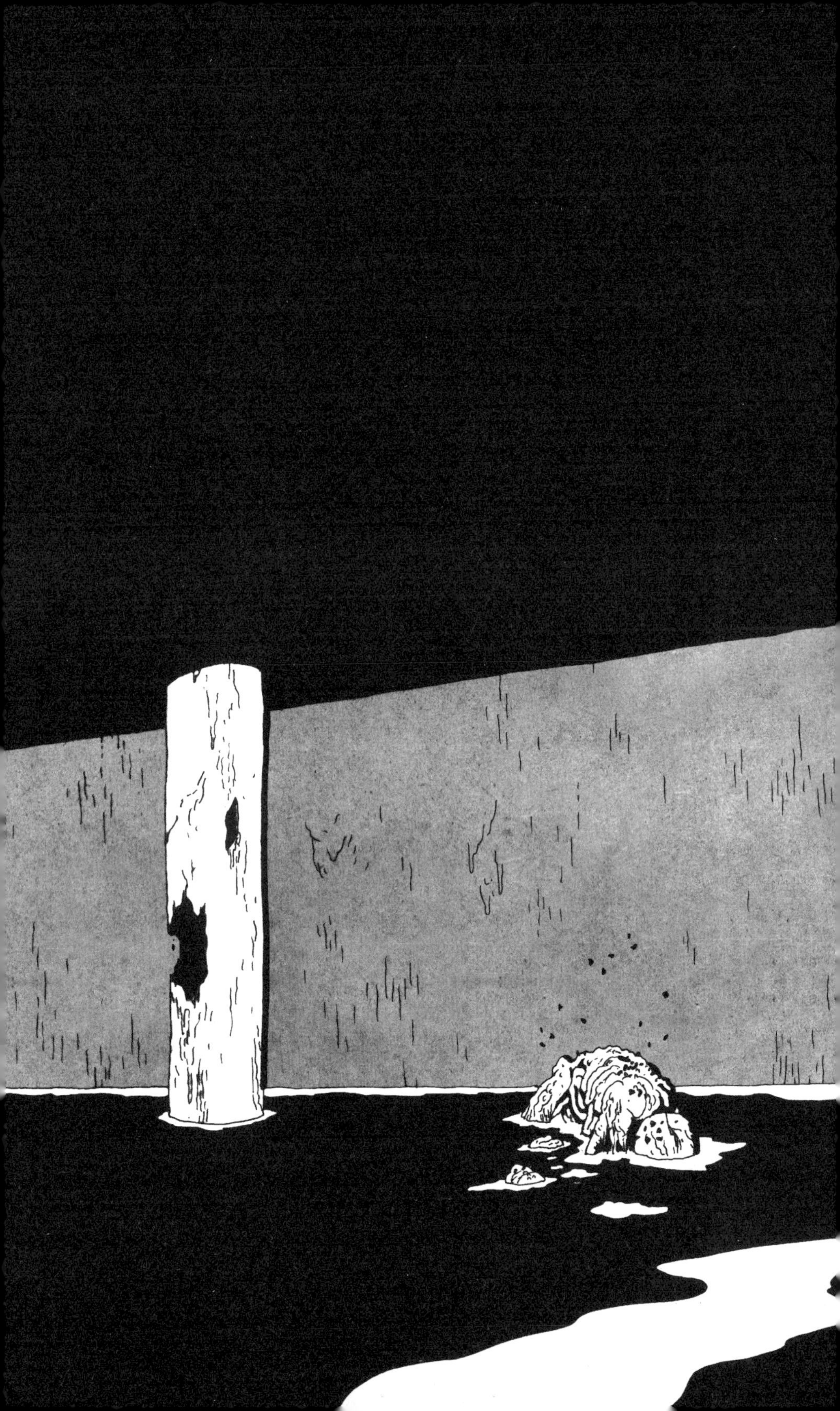

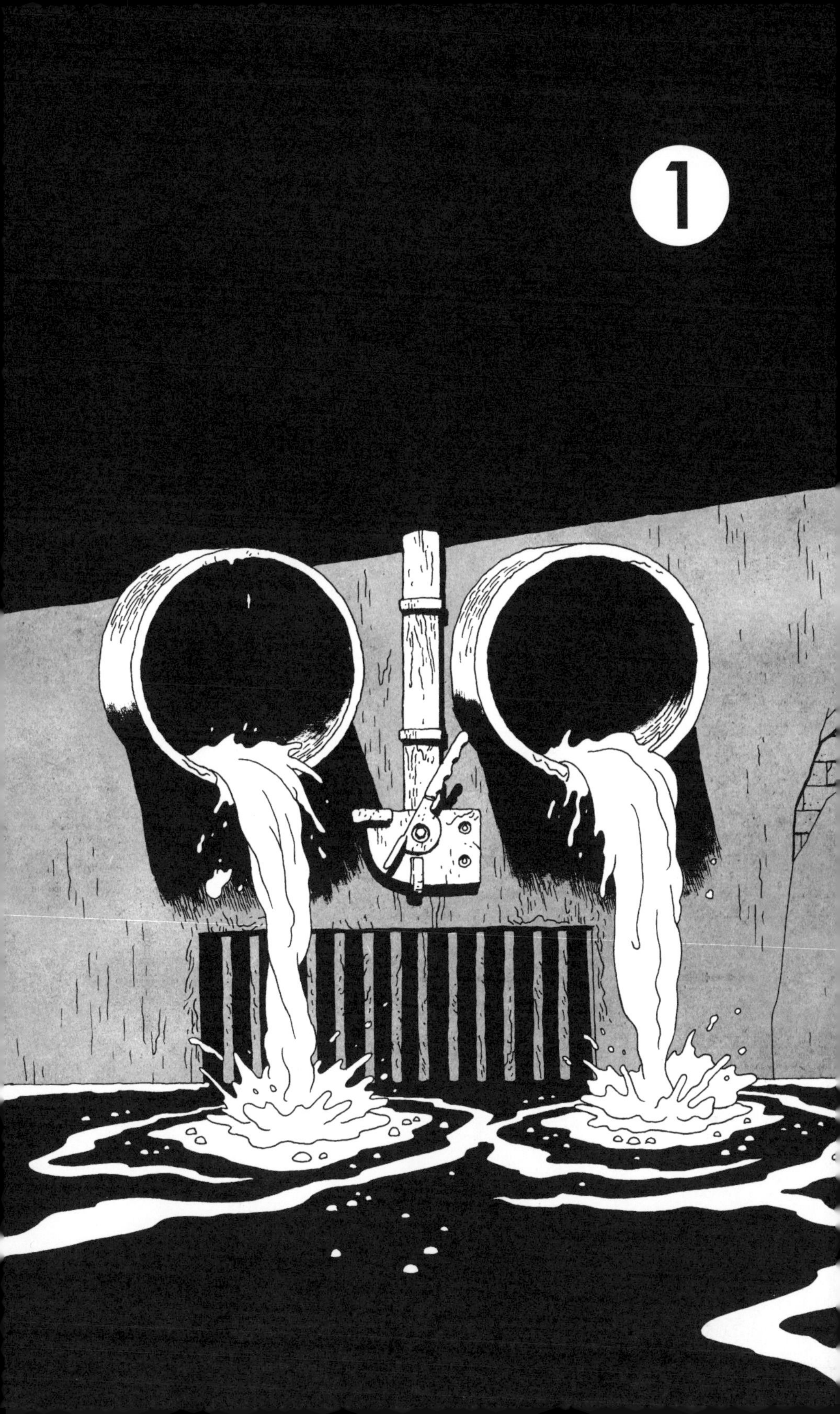
1

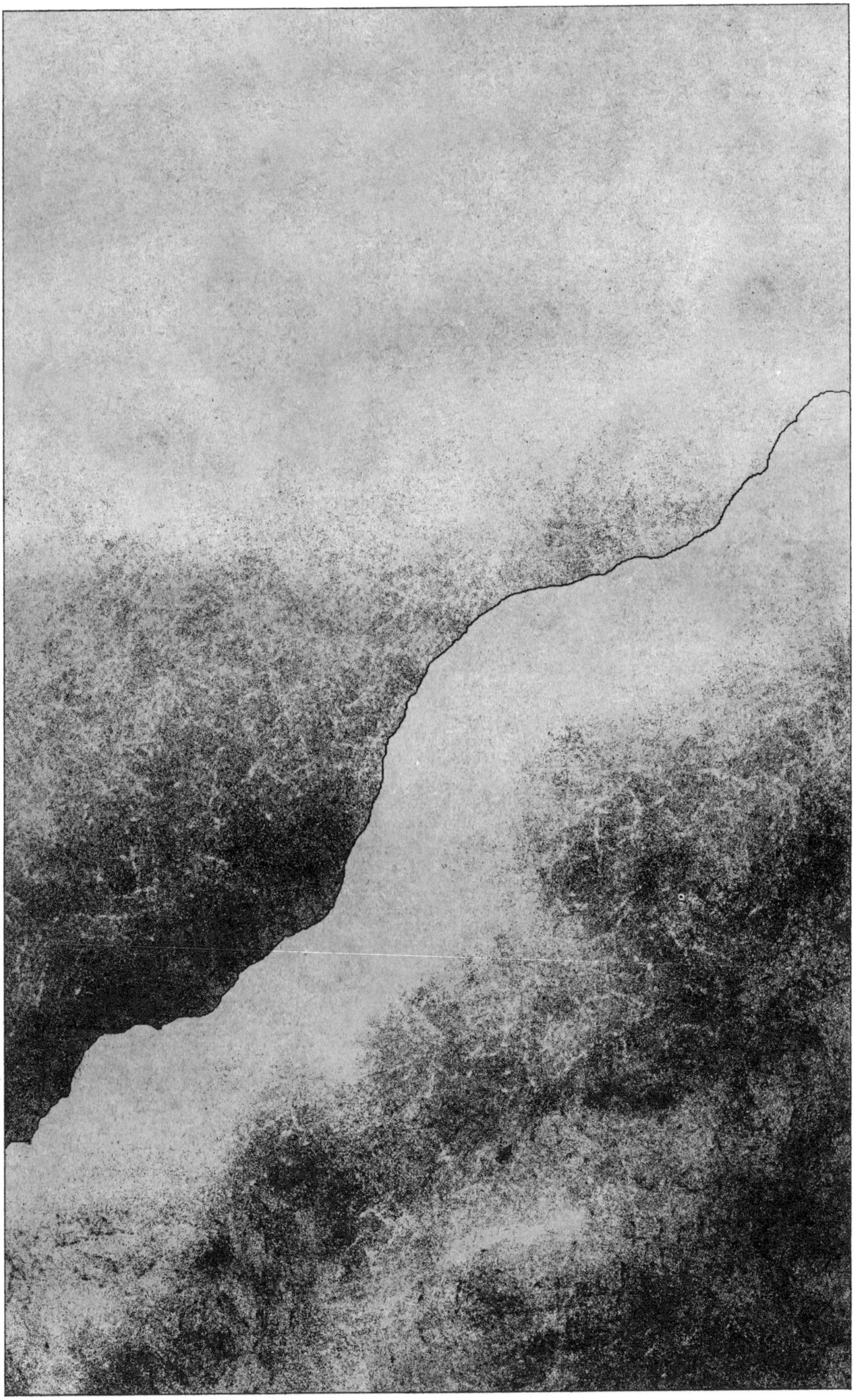

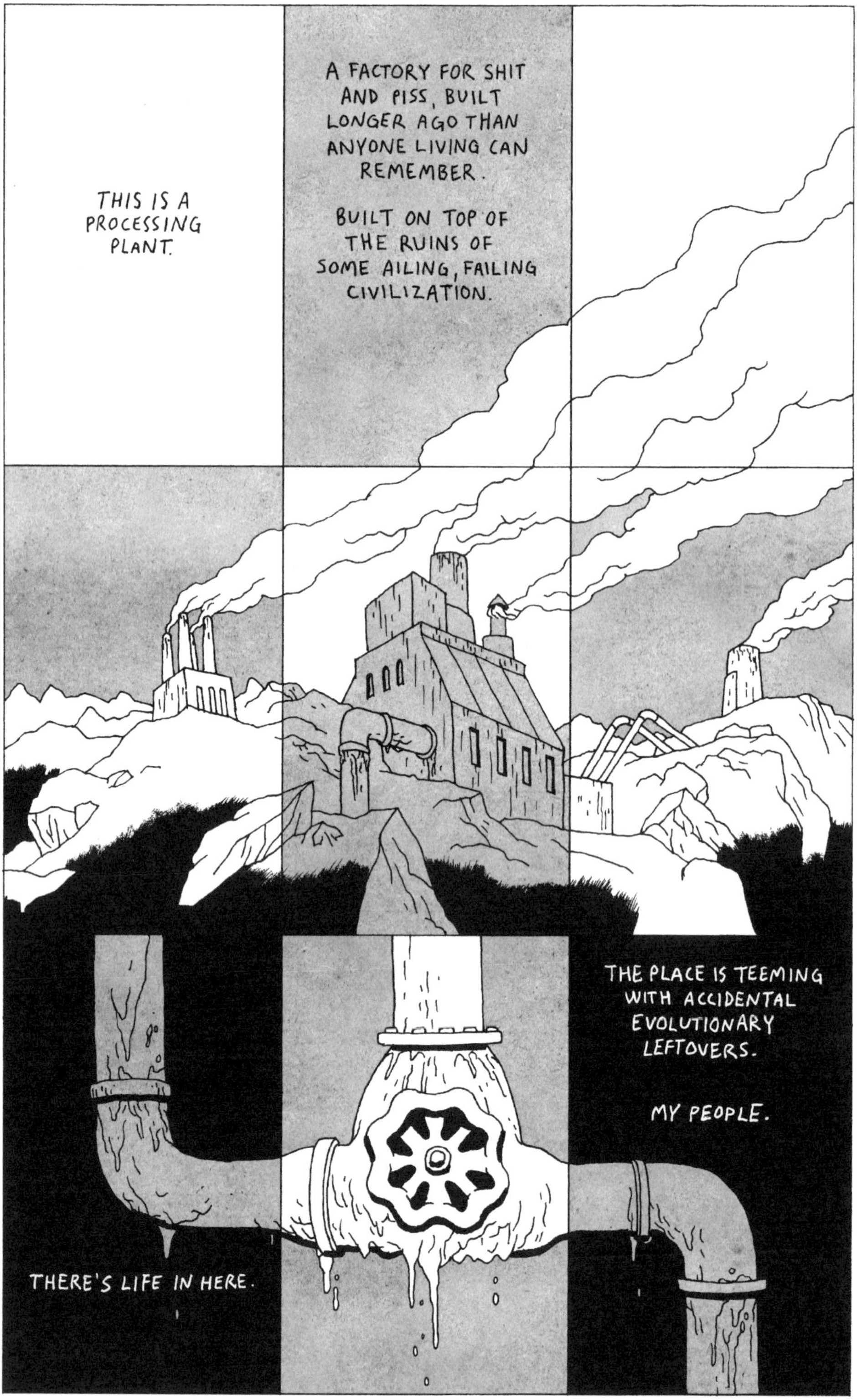
THIS IS A PROCESSING PLANT.
A FACTORY FOR SHIT AND PISS, BUILT LONGER AGO THAN ANYONE LIVING CAN REMEMBER.
BUILT ON TOP OF THE RUINS OF SOME AILING, FAILING CIVILIZATION.
THERE'S LIFE IN HERE.
THE PLACE IS TEEMING WITH ACCIDENTAL EVOLUTIONARY LEFTOVERS.
MY PEOPLE.

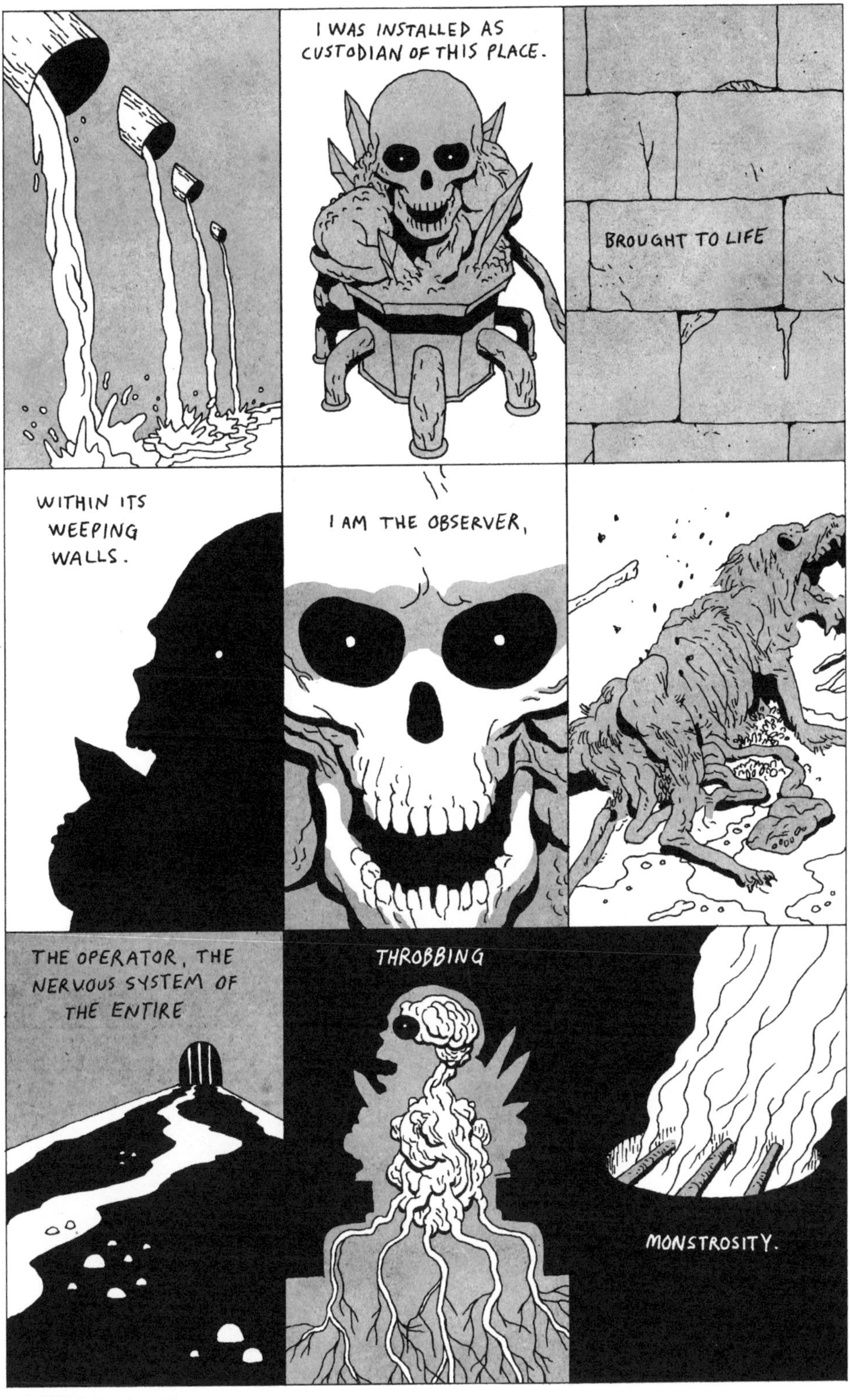
I WAS INSTALLED AS CUSTODIAN OF THIS PLACE.
BROUGHT TO LIFE
WITHIN ITS WEEPING WALLS.
I AM THE OBSERVER,
THE OPERATOR, THE NERVOUS SYSTEM OF THE ENTIRE
THROBBING
MONSTROSITY.

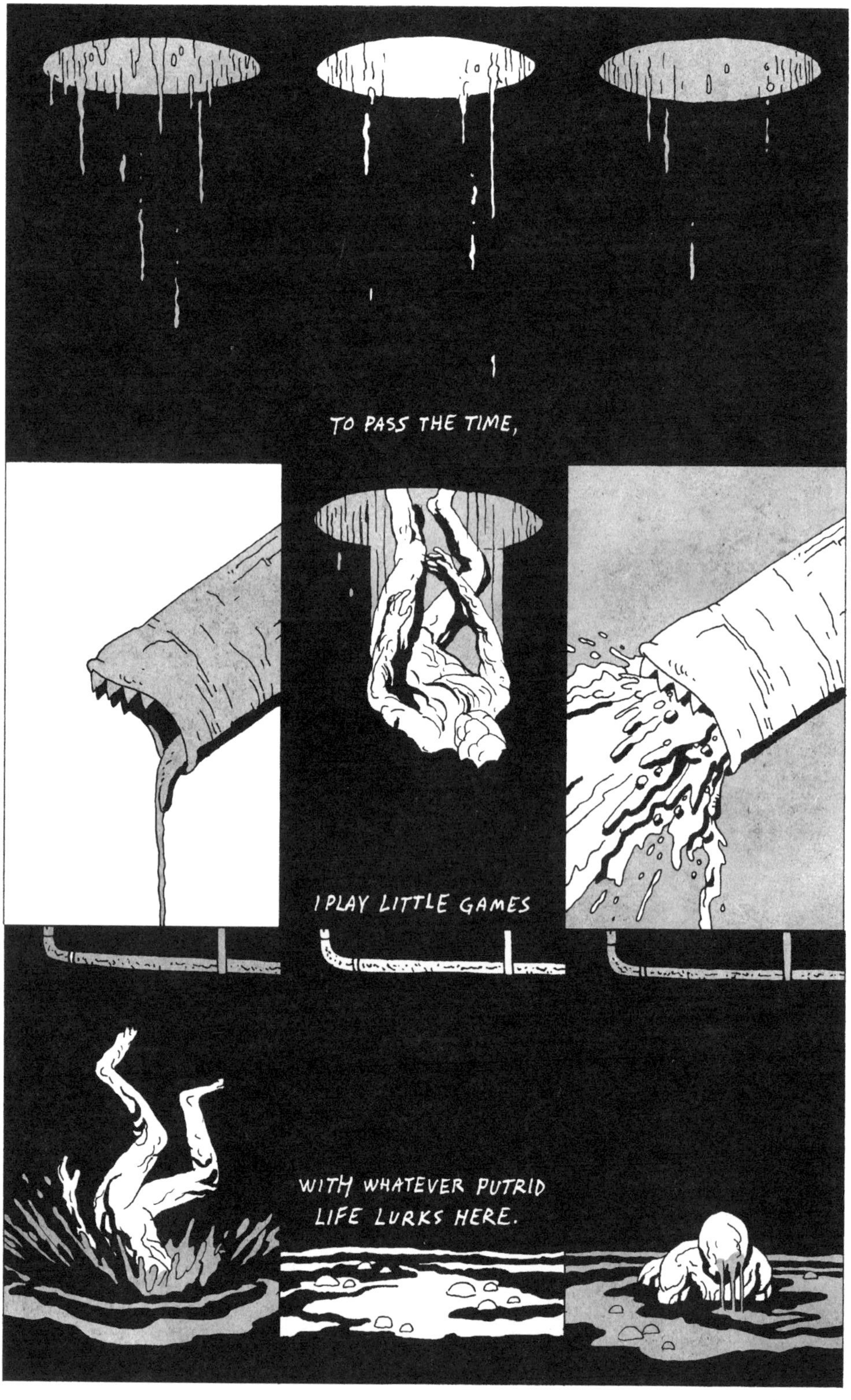
TO PASS THE TIME,
I PLAY LITTLE GAMES
WITH WHATEVER PUTRID LIFE LURKS HERE.

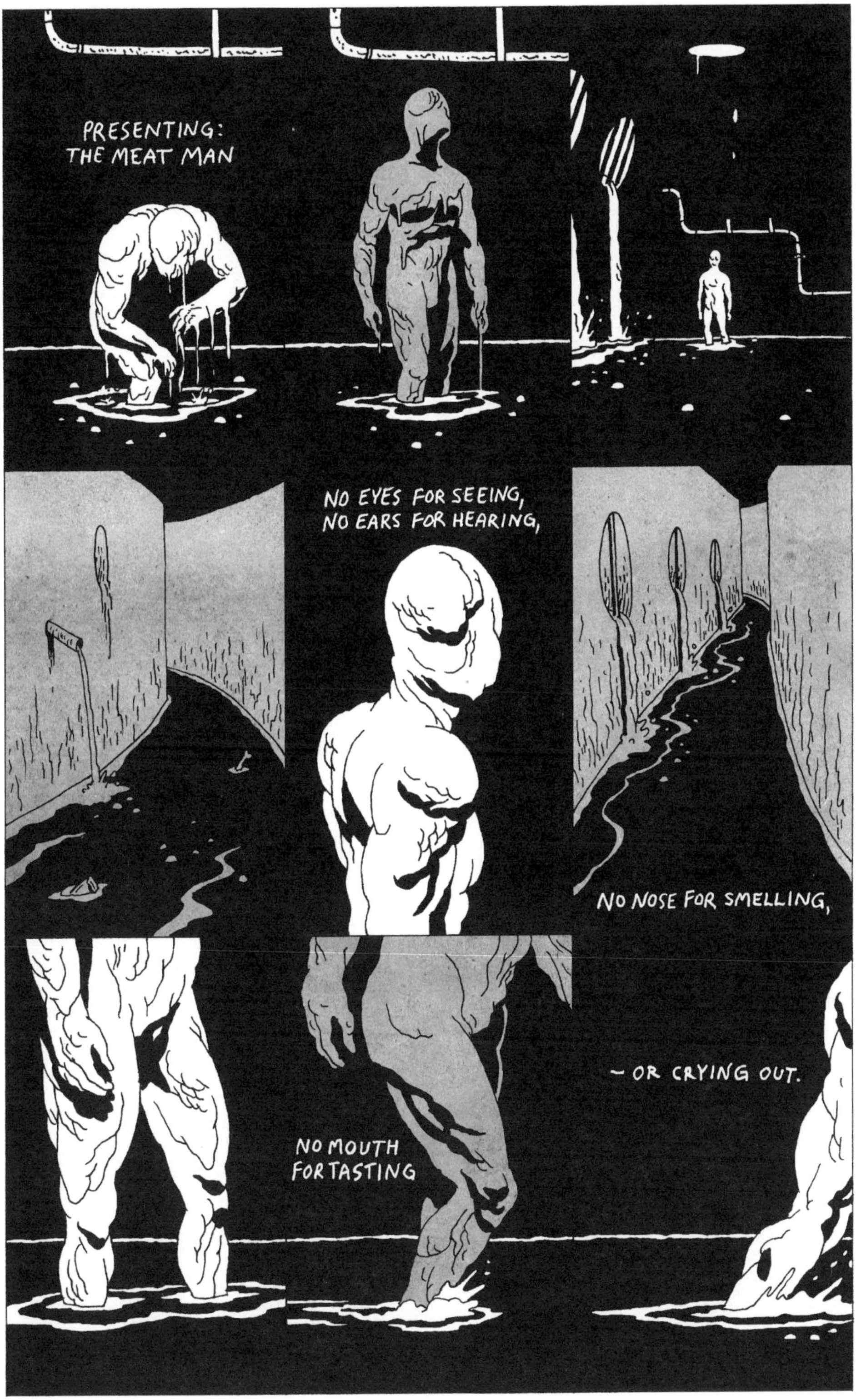
PRESENTING:
THE MEAT MAN
NO EYES FOR SEEING,
NO EARS FOR HEARING,
NO NOSE FOR SMELLING,
NO MOUTH
FOR TASTING
– OR CRYING OUT.

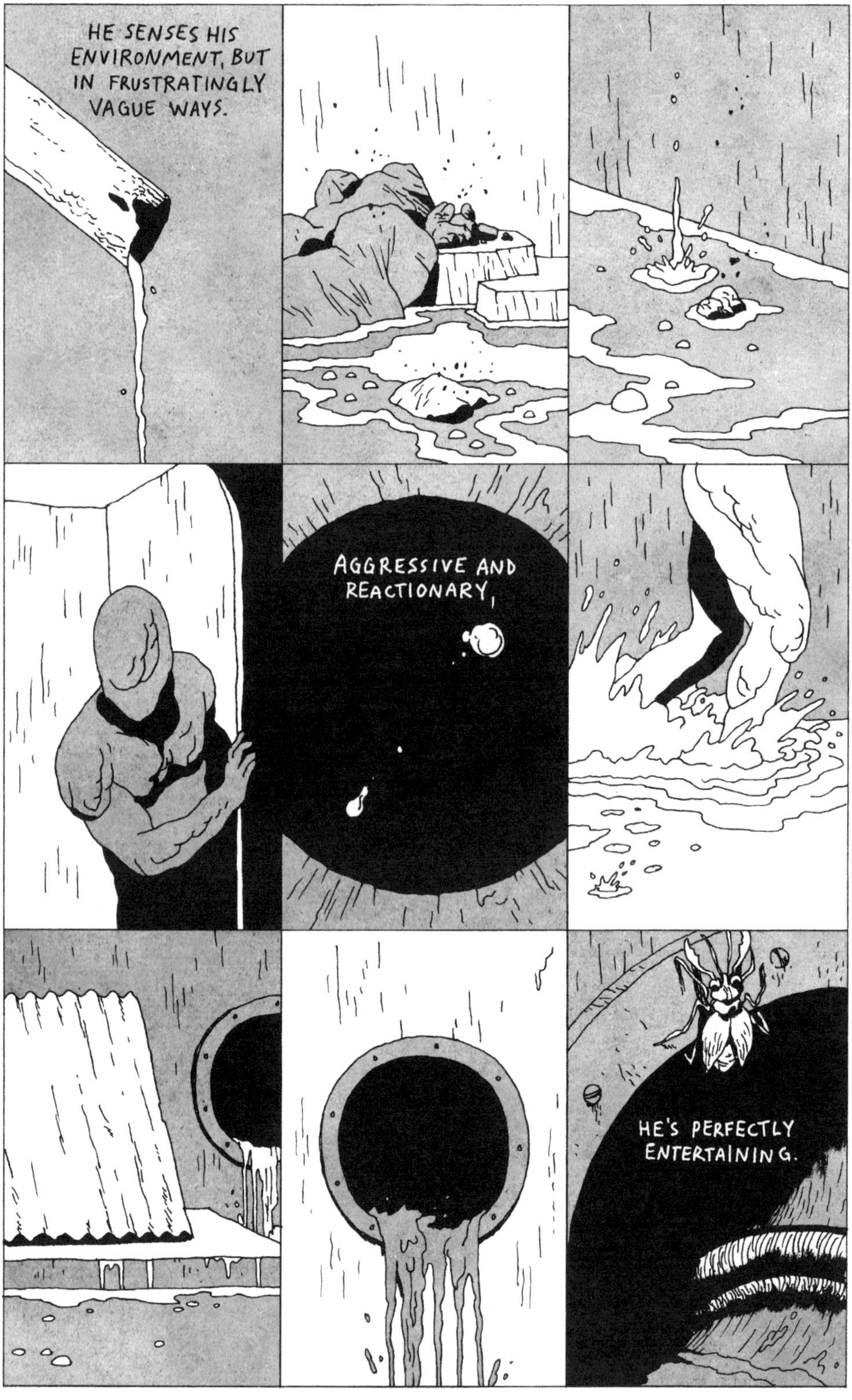
HE SENSES HIS ENVIRONMENT, BUT IN FRUSTRATINGLY VAGUE WAYS.
AGGRESSIVE AND REACTIONARY,
HE'S PERFECTLY ENTERTAINING.

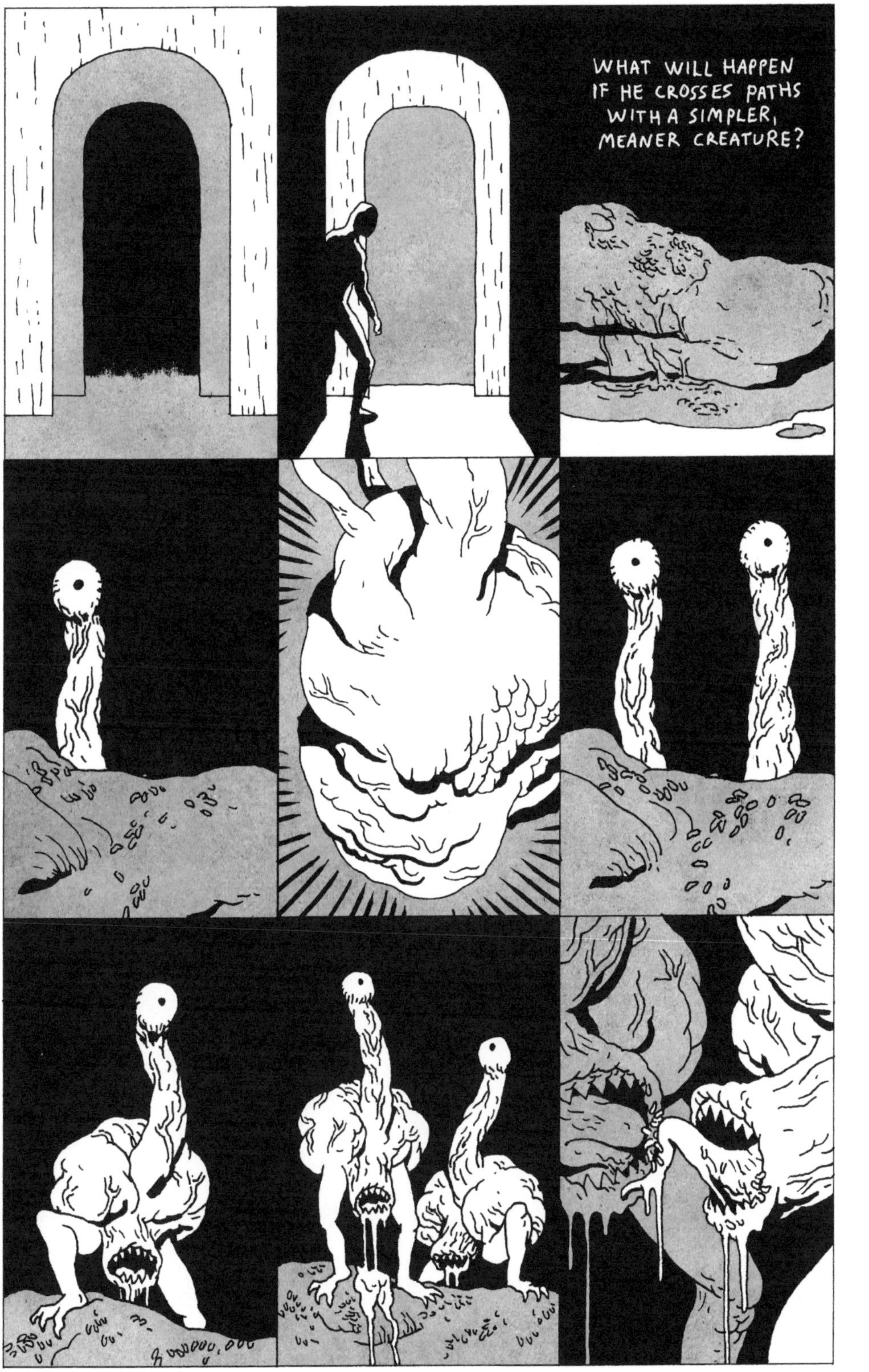
WHAT WILL HAPPEN IF HE CROSSES PATHS WITH A SIMPLER, MEANER CREATURE?

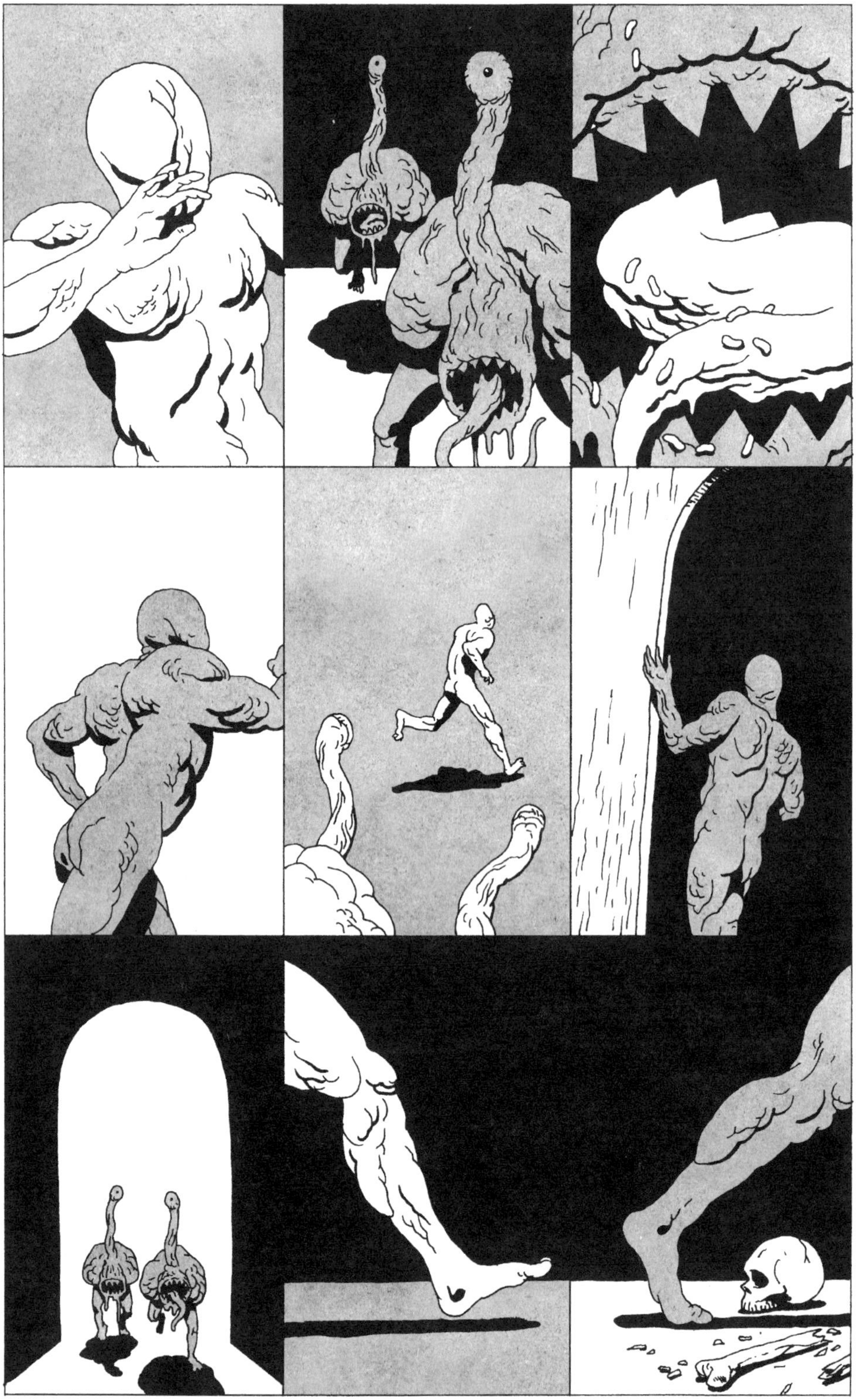

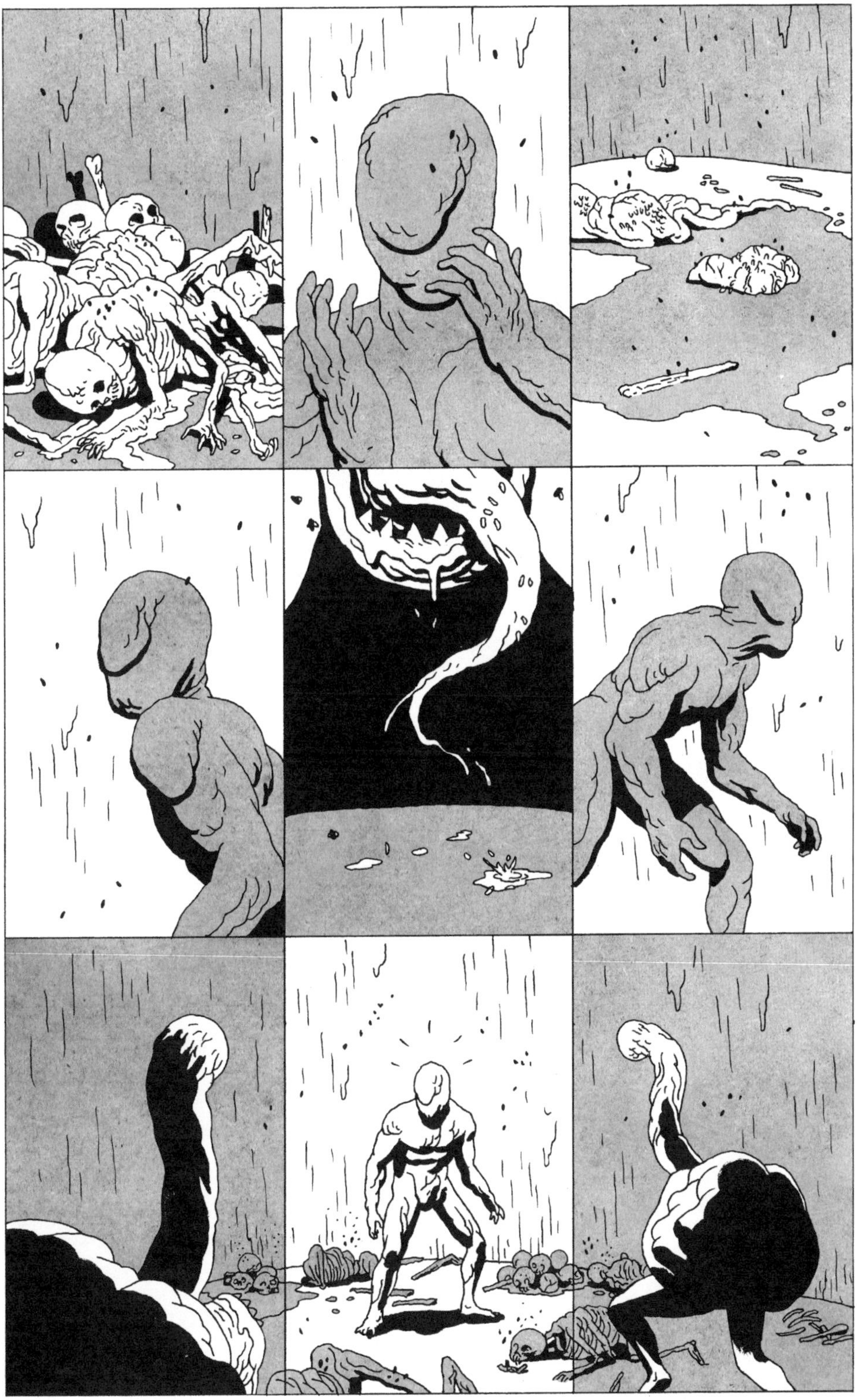

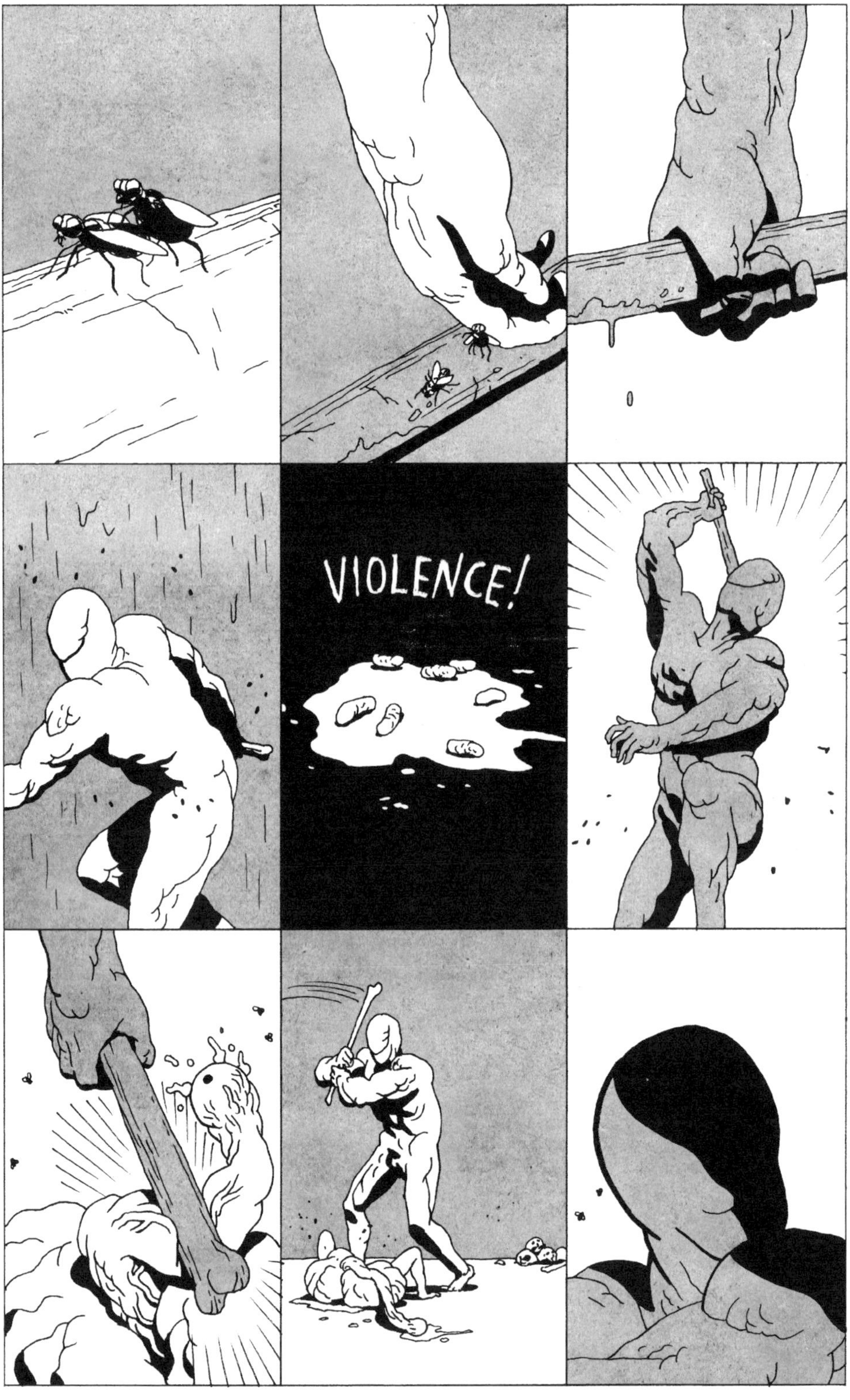
VIOLENCE!

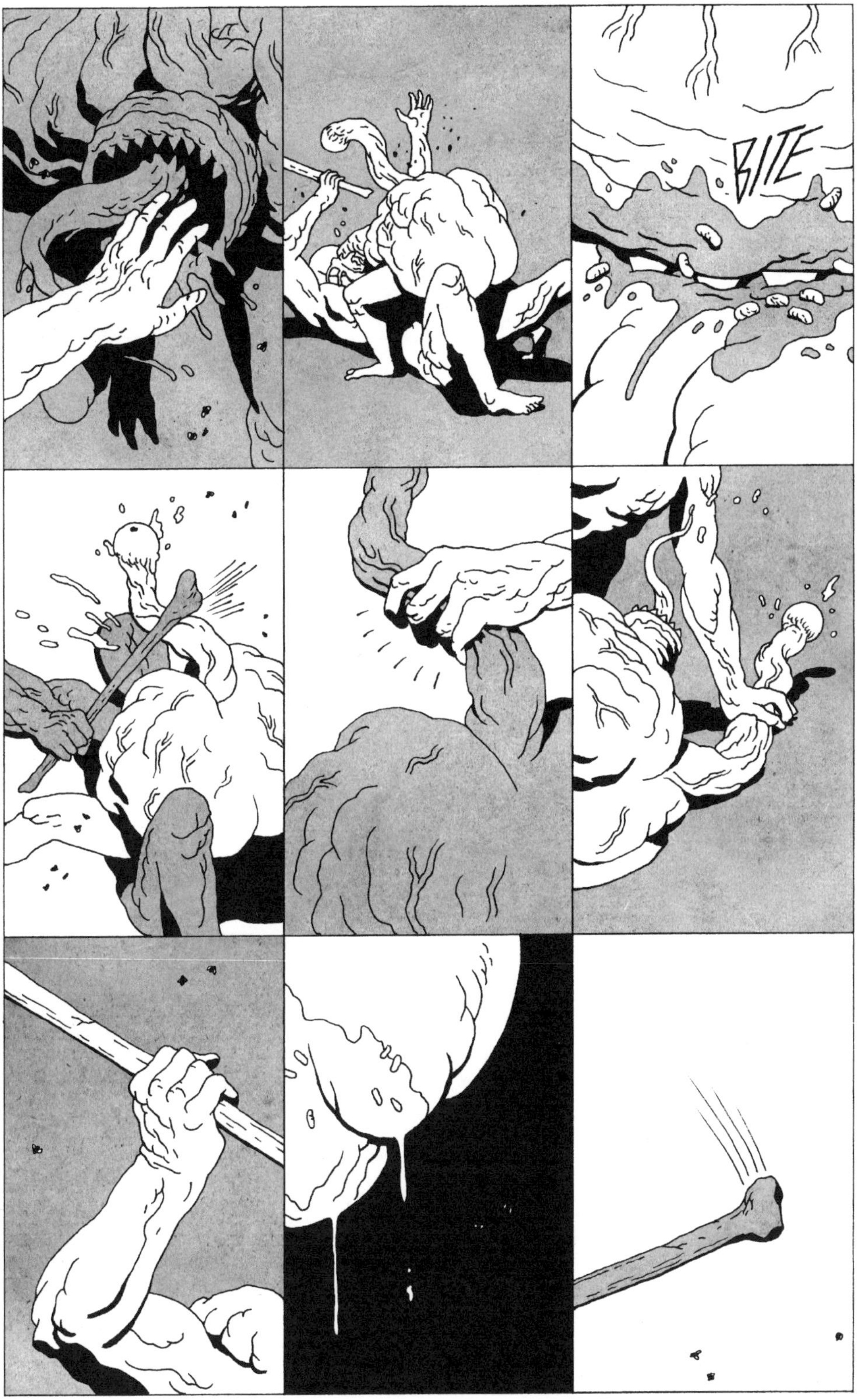
BITE

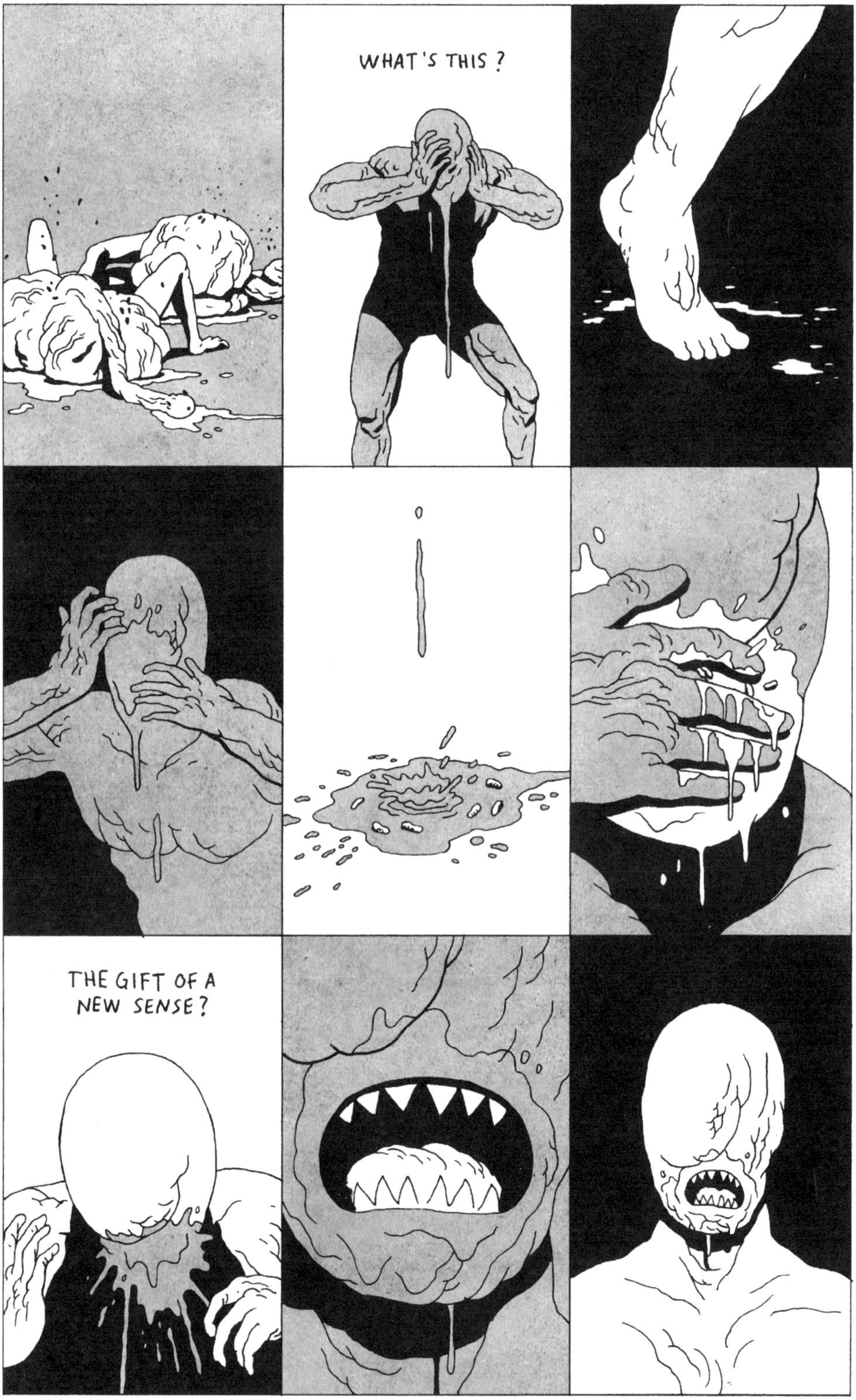
WHAT'S THIS?
THE GIFT OF A NEW SENSE?

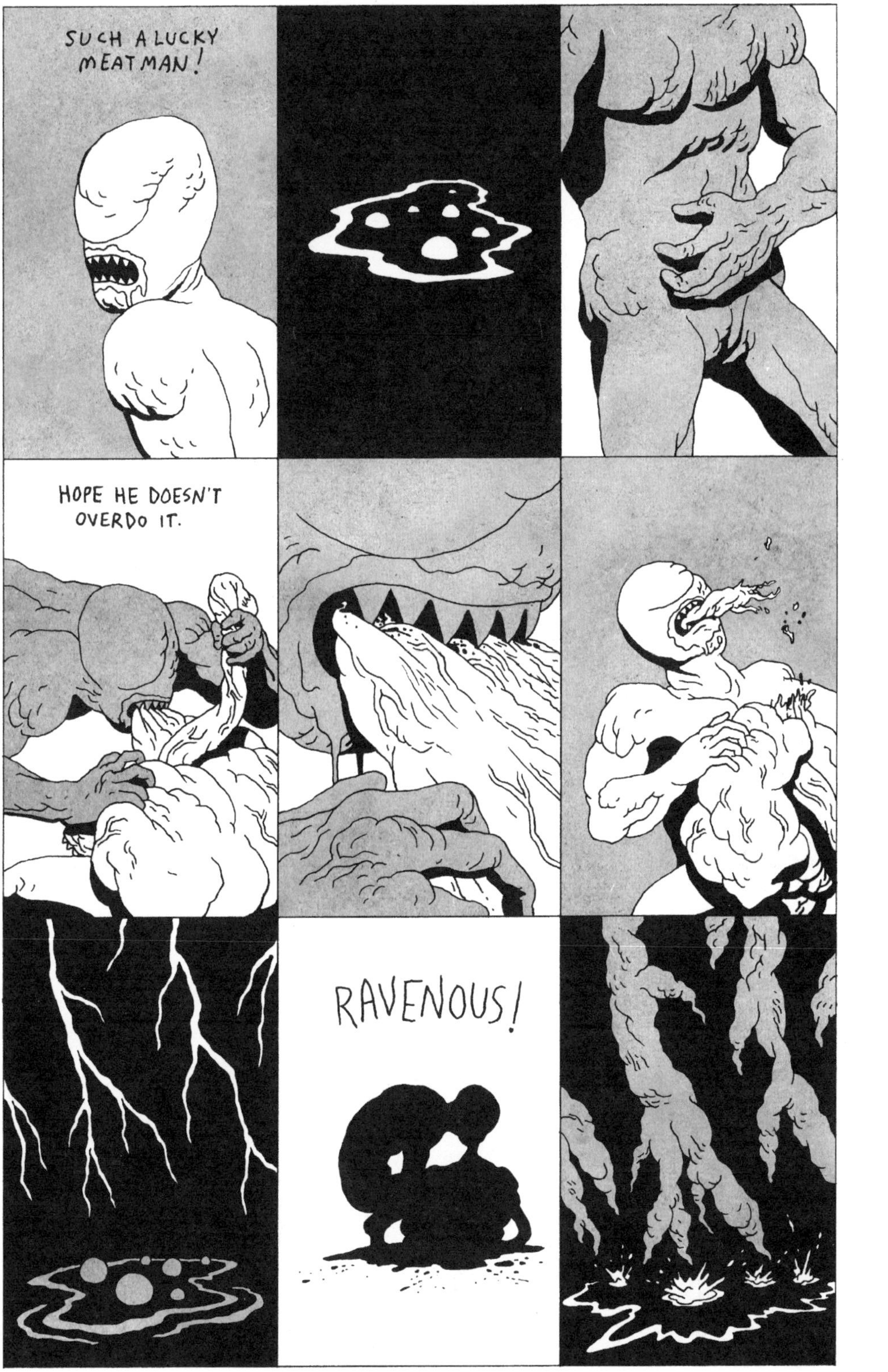
SUCH A LUCKY MEATMAN!
HOPE HE DOESN'T OVERDO IT.
RAVENOUS!

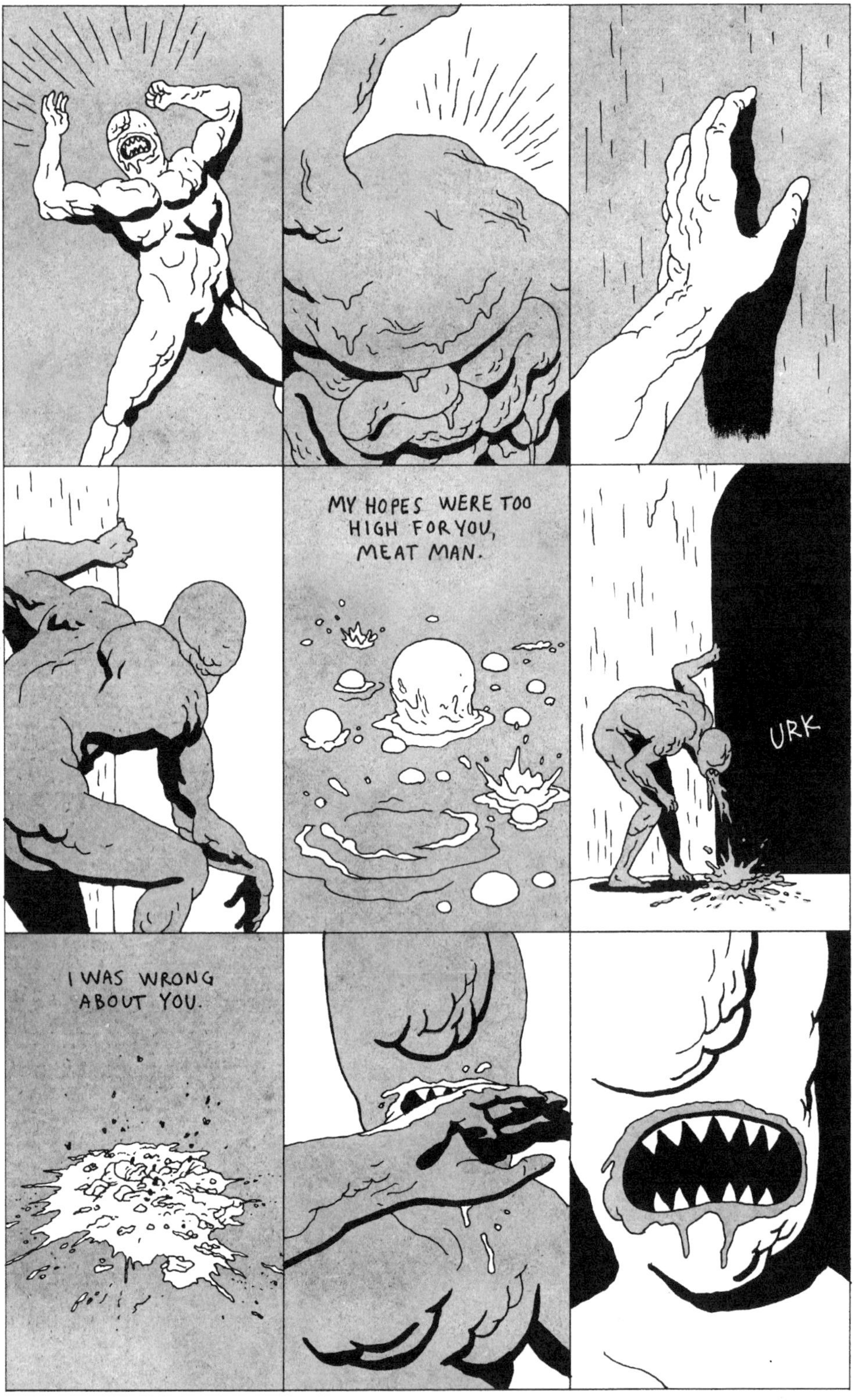
MY HOPES WERE TOO HIGH FOR YOU, MEAT MAN.
URK
I WAS WRONG ABOUT YOU.

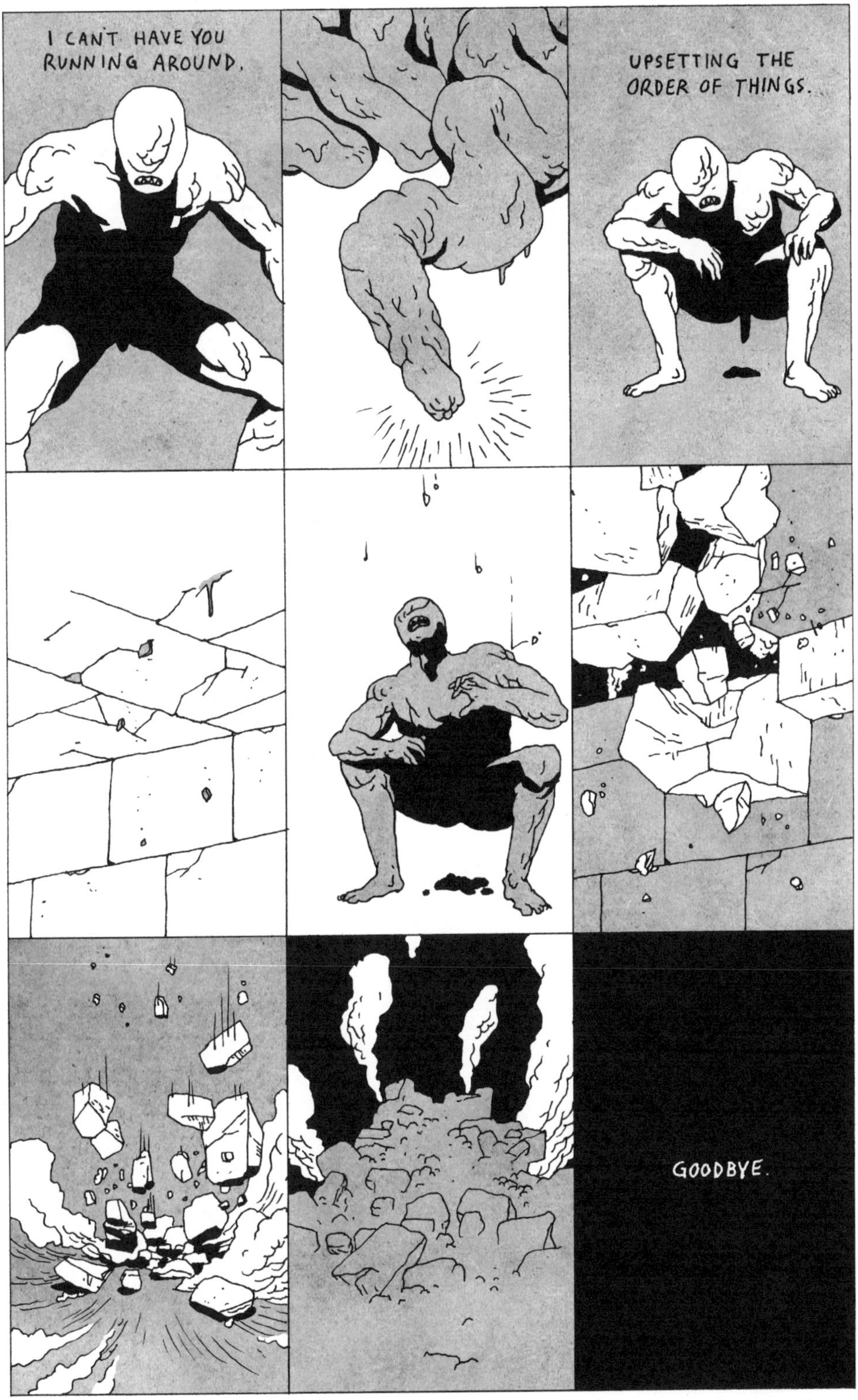
I CAN'T HAVE YOU RUNNING AROUND.
UPSETTING THE ORDER OF THINGS.
GOODBYE.

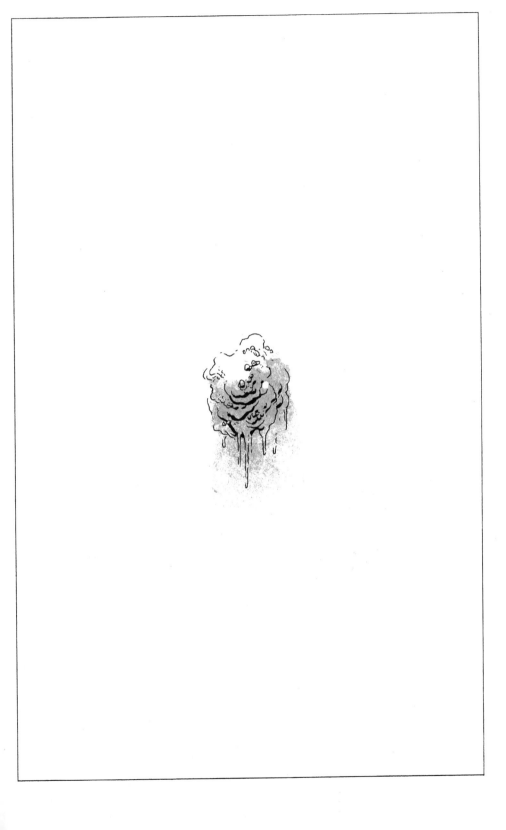

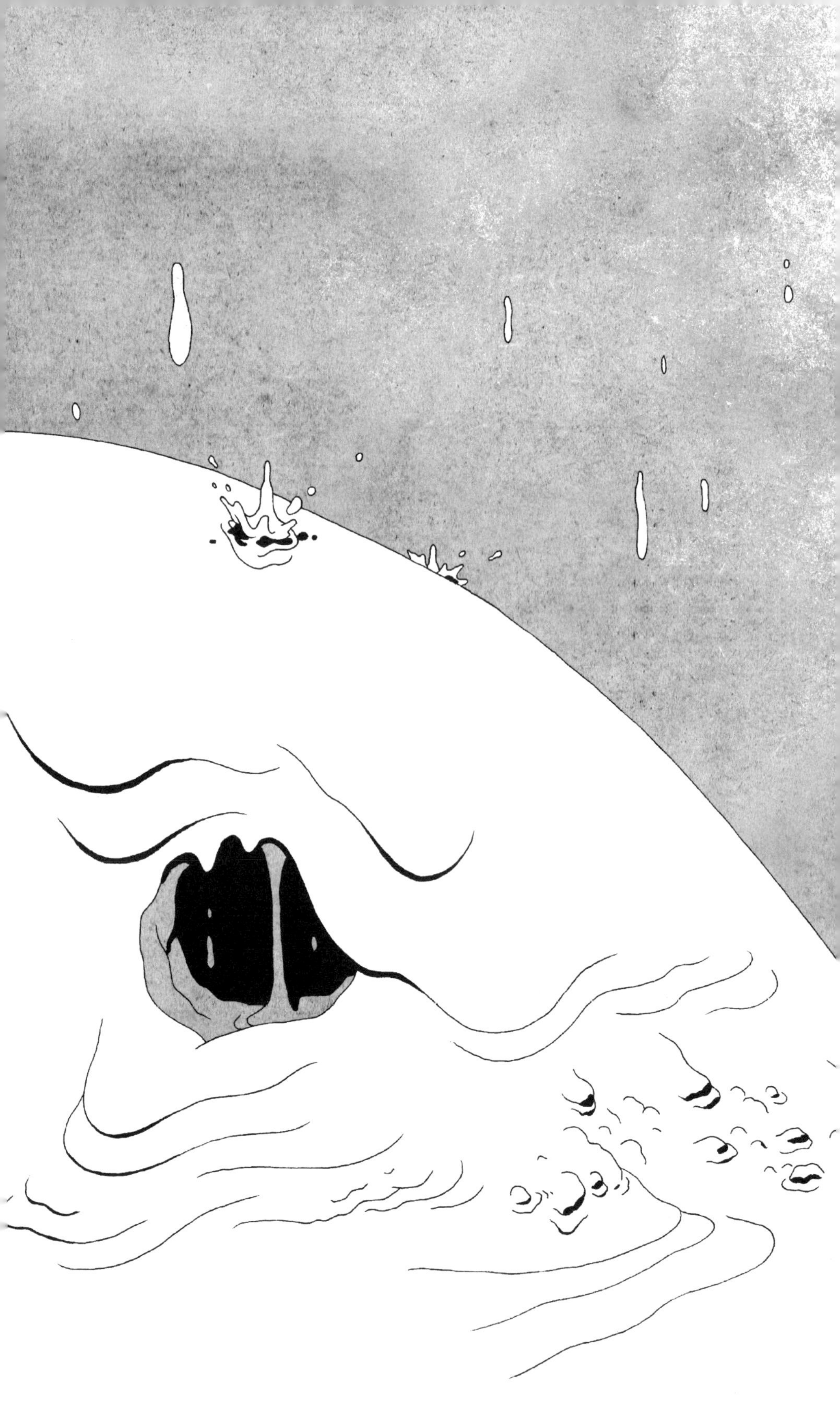

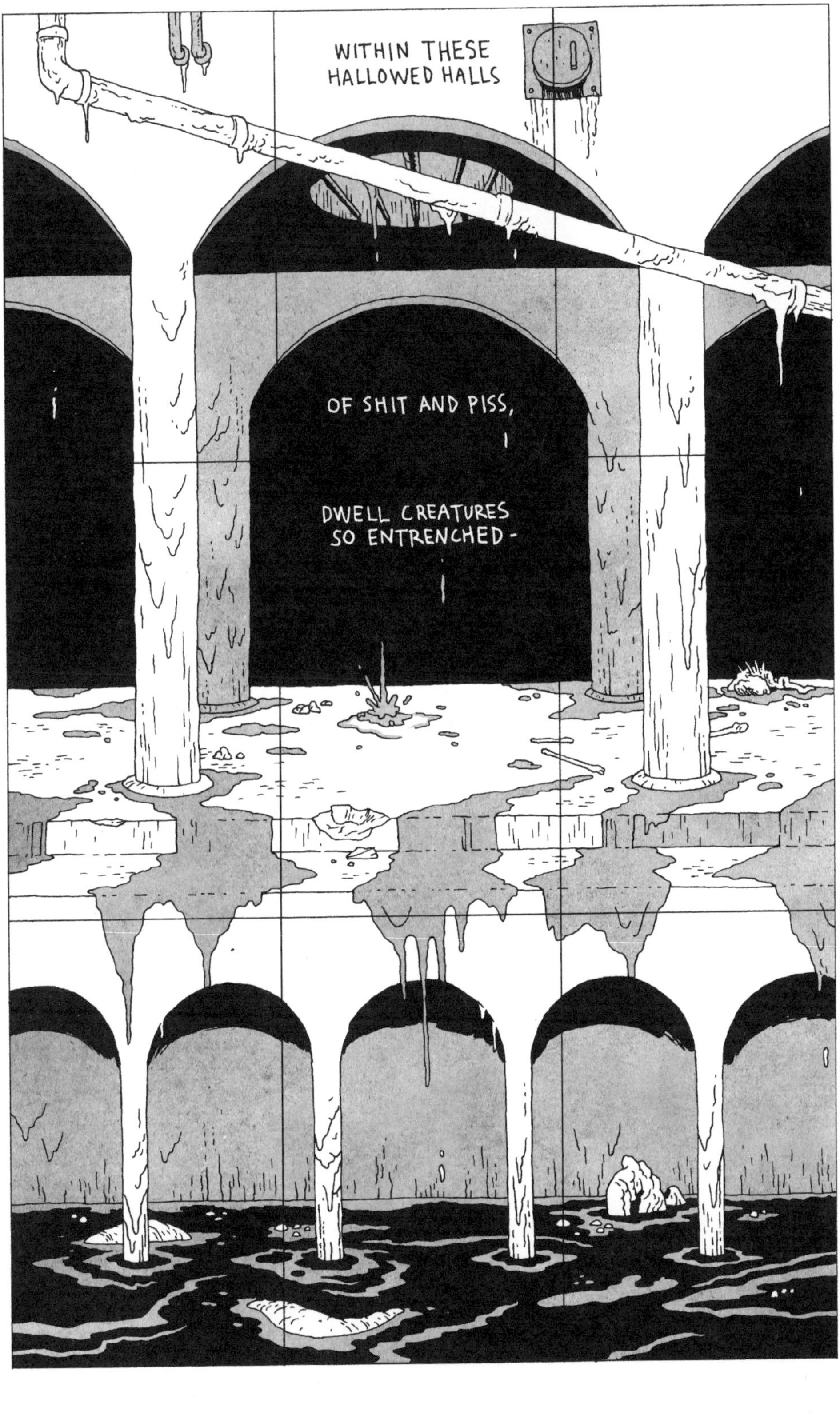
WITHIN THESE HALLOWED HALLS
OF SHIT AND PISS,
DWELL CREATURES SO ENTRENCHED -

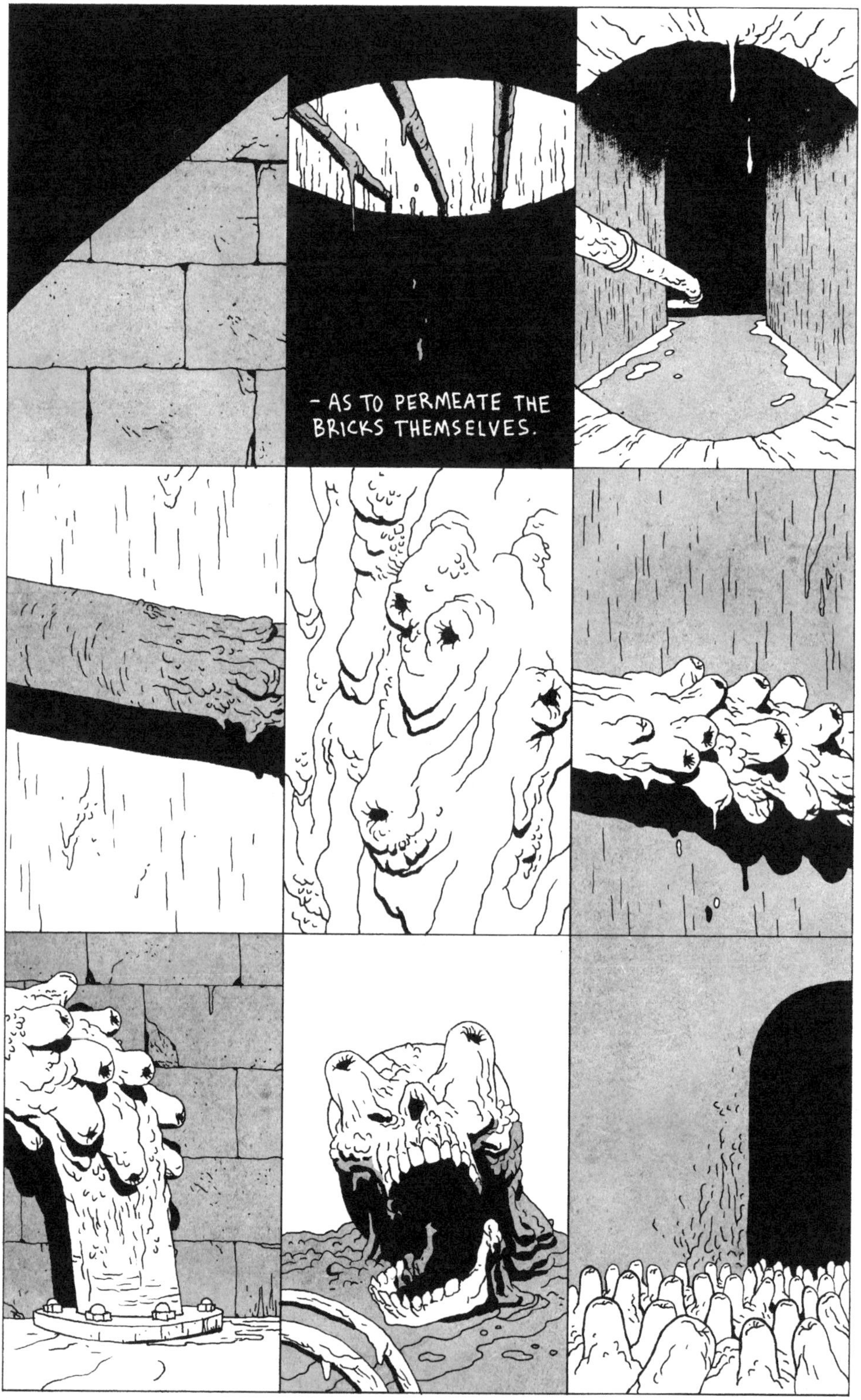
- AS TO PERMEATE THE BRICKS THEMSELVES.

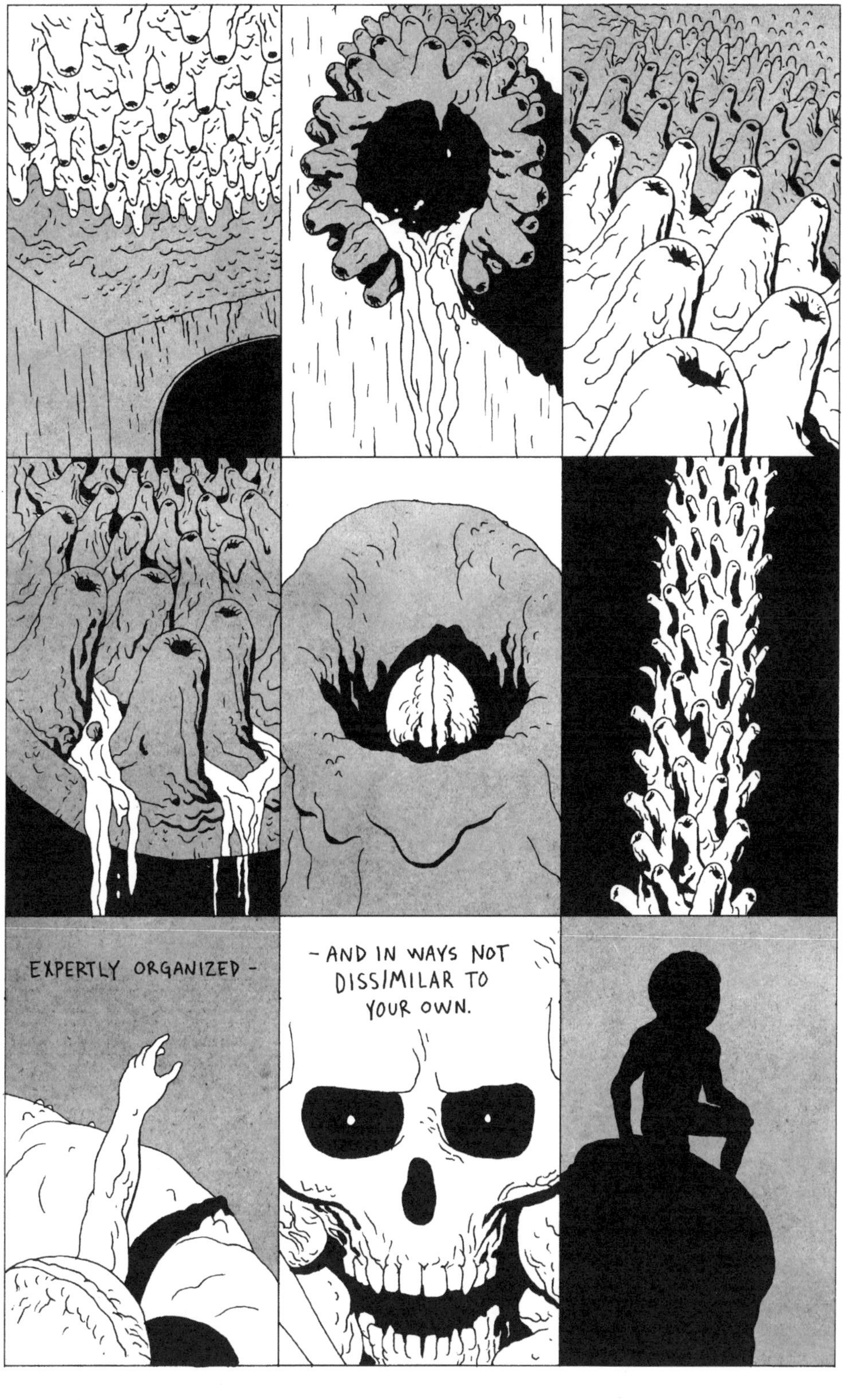
EXPERTLY ORGANIZED -
- AND IN WAYS NOT DISSIMILAR TO YOUR OWN.

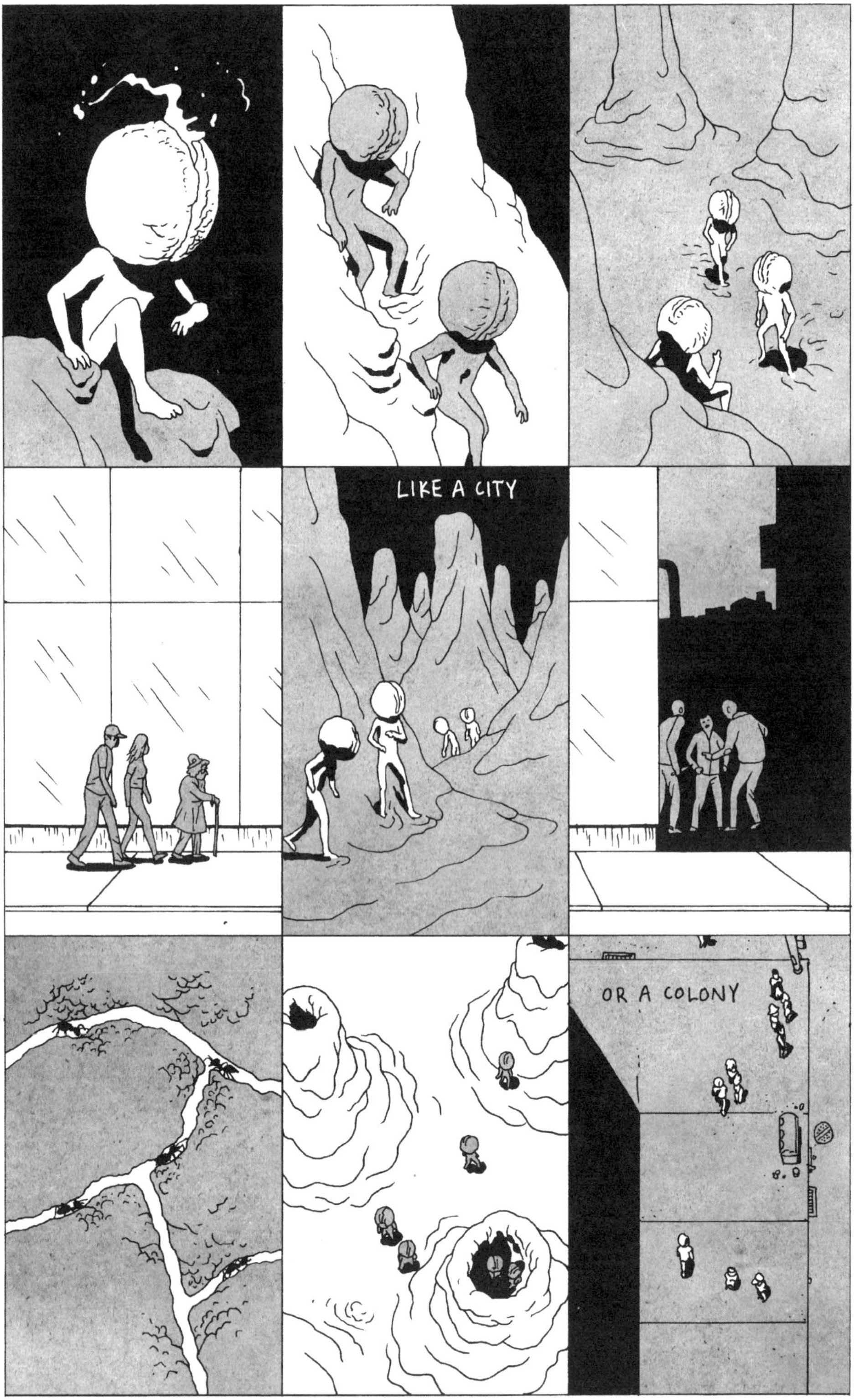
LIKE A CITY
OR A COLONY

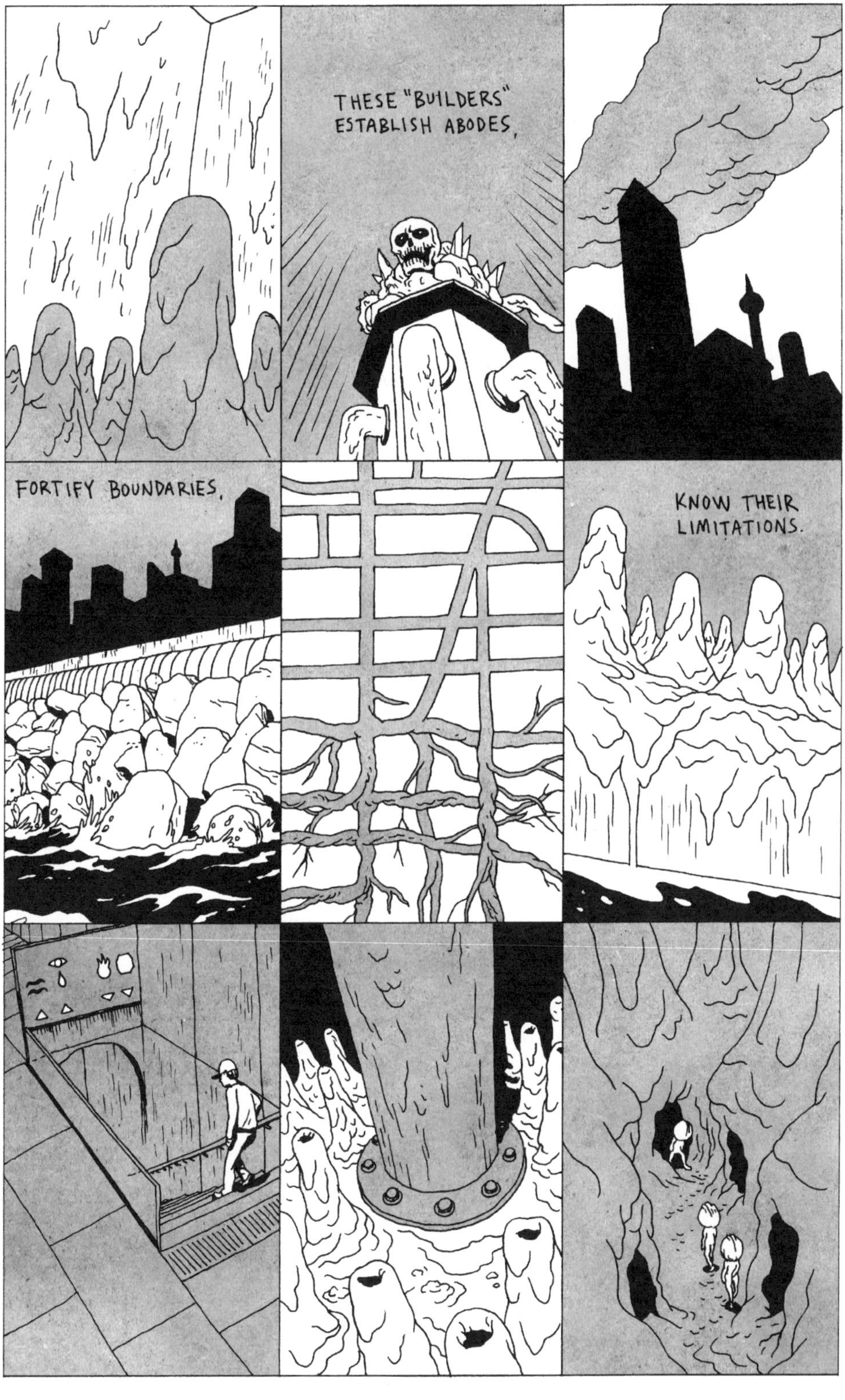
THESE "BUILDERS" ESTABLISH ABODES,
FORTIFY BOUNDARIES,
KNOW THEIR LIMITATIONS.

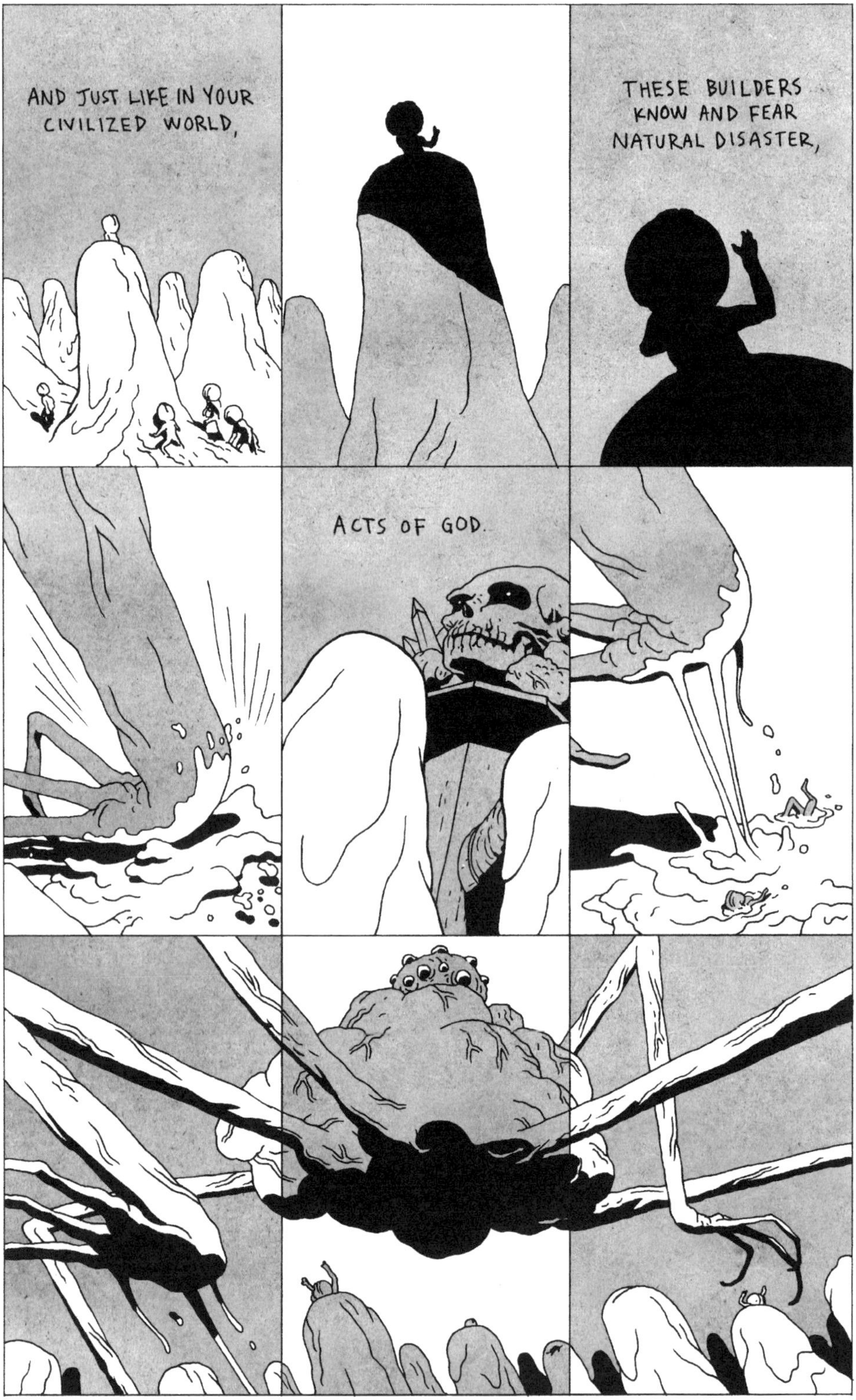
AND JUST LIKE IN YOUR CIVILIZED WORLD,
THESE BUILDERS KNOW AND FEAR NATURAL DISASTER,
ACTS OF GOD.

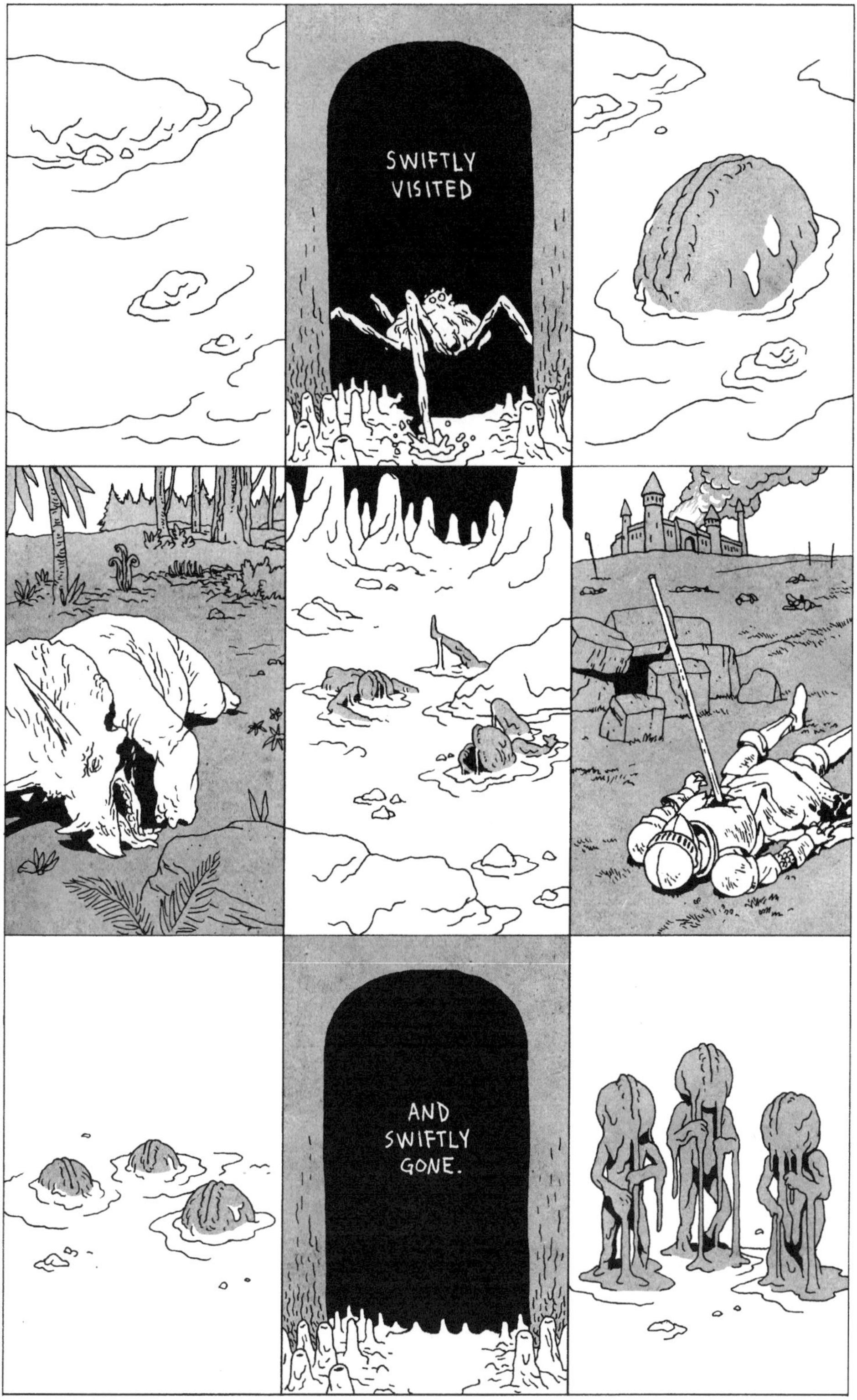
SWIFTLY VISITED
AND SWIFTLY GONE.

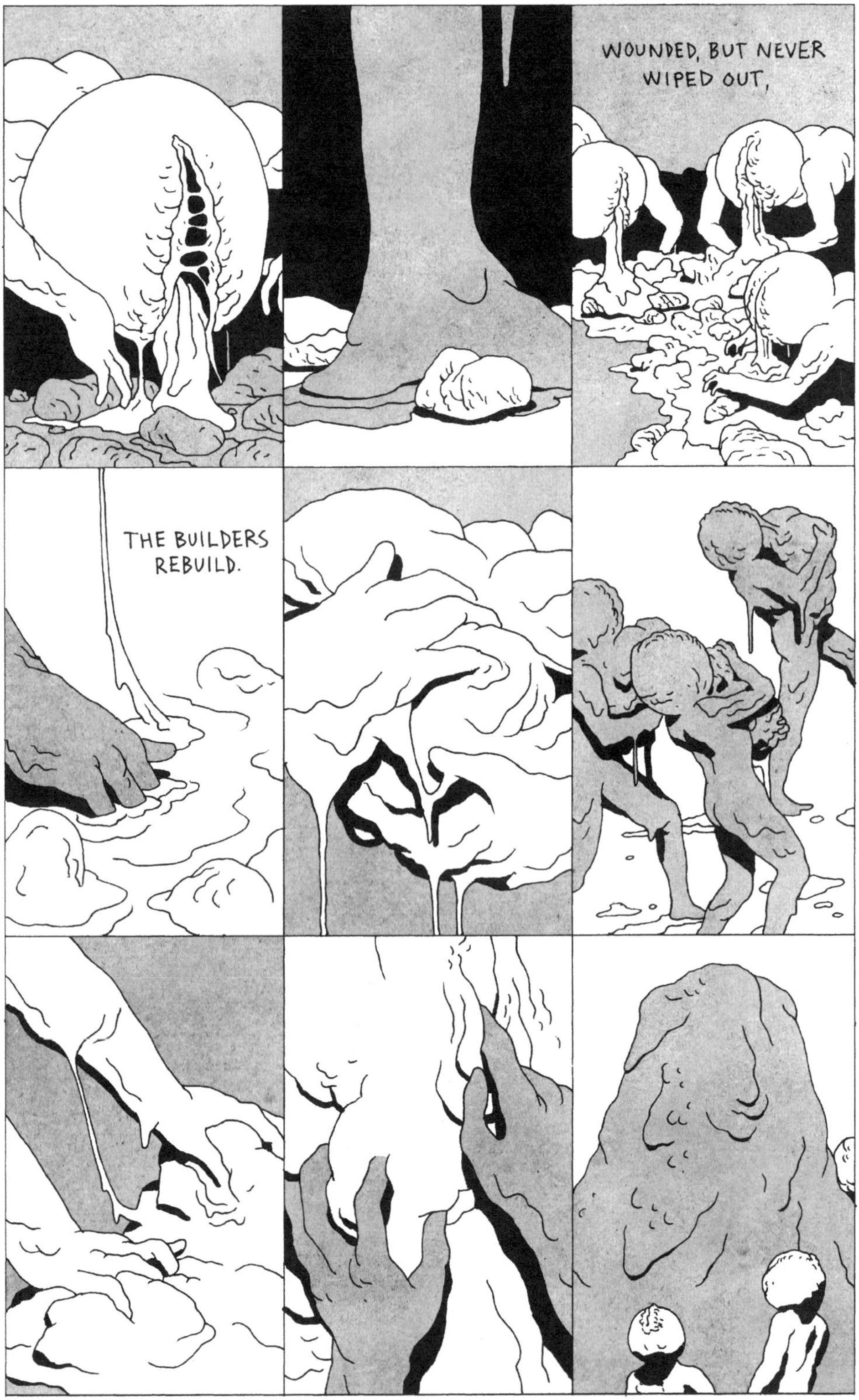
WOUNDED, BUT NEVER WIPED OUT,
THE BUILDERS REBUILD.

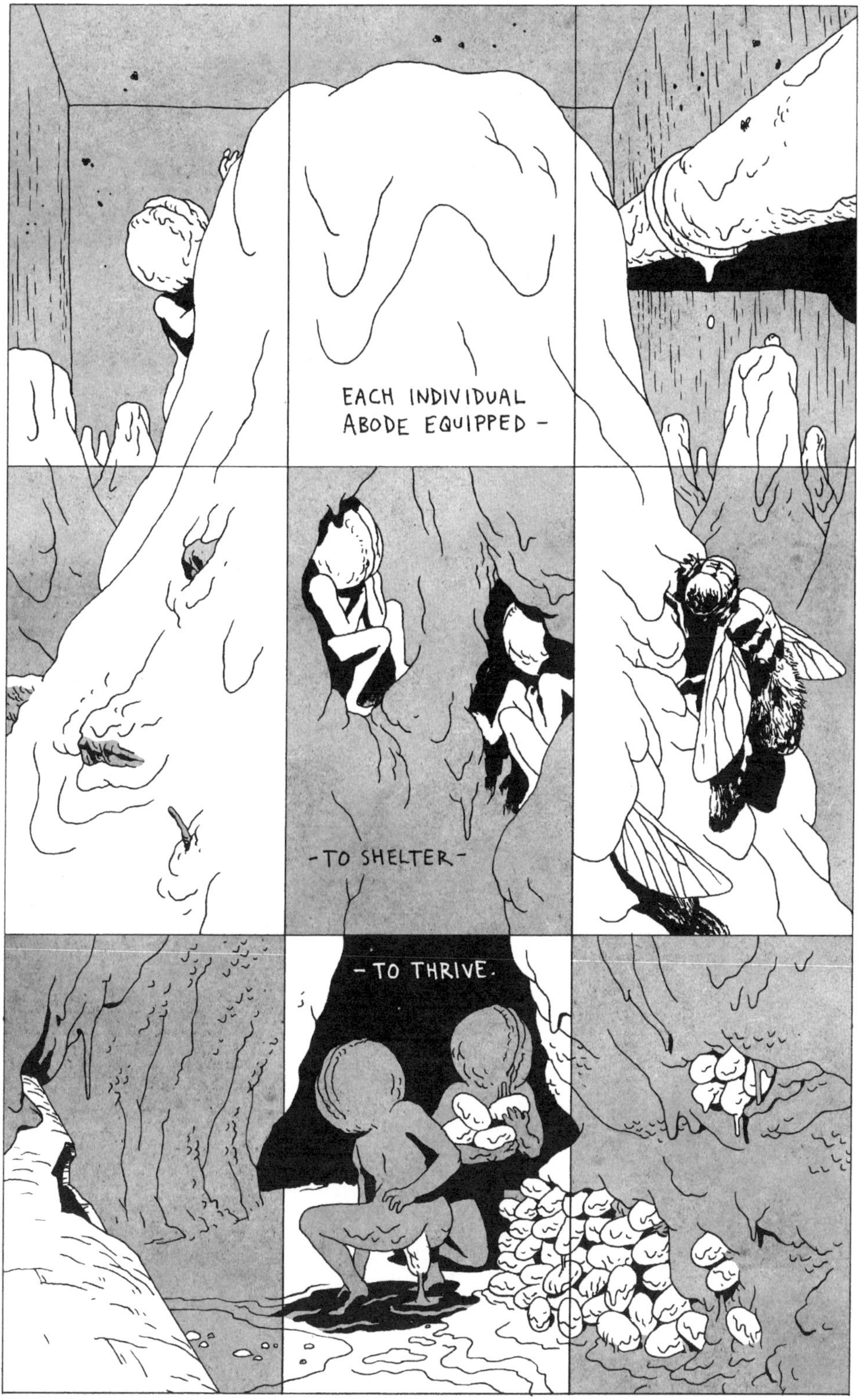
EACH INDIVIDUAL ABODE EQUIPPED -
-TO SHELTER-
-TO THRIVE.

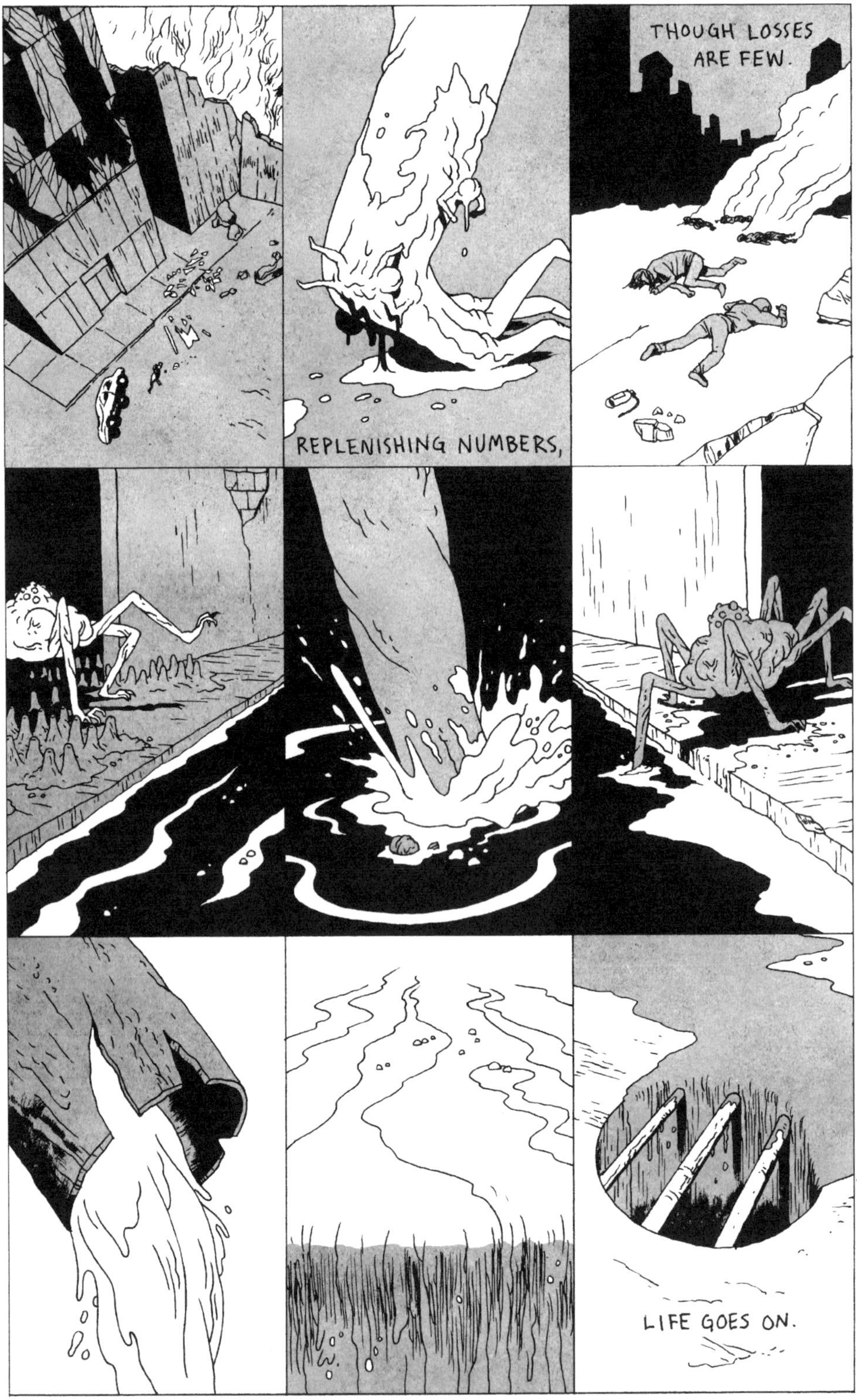
REPLENISHING NUMBERS,
THOUGH LOSSES ARE FEW.
LIFE GOES ON.

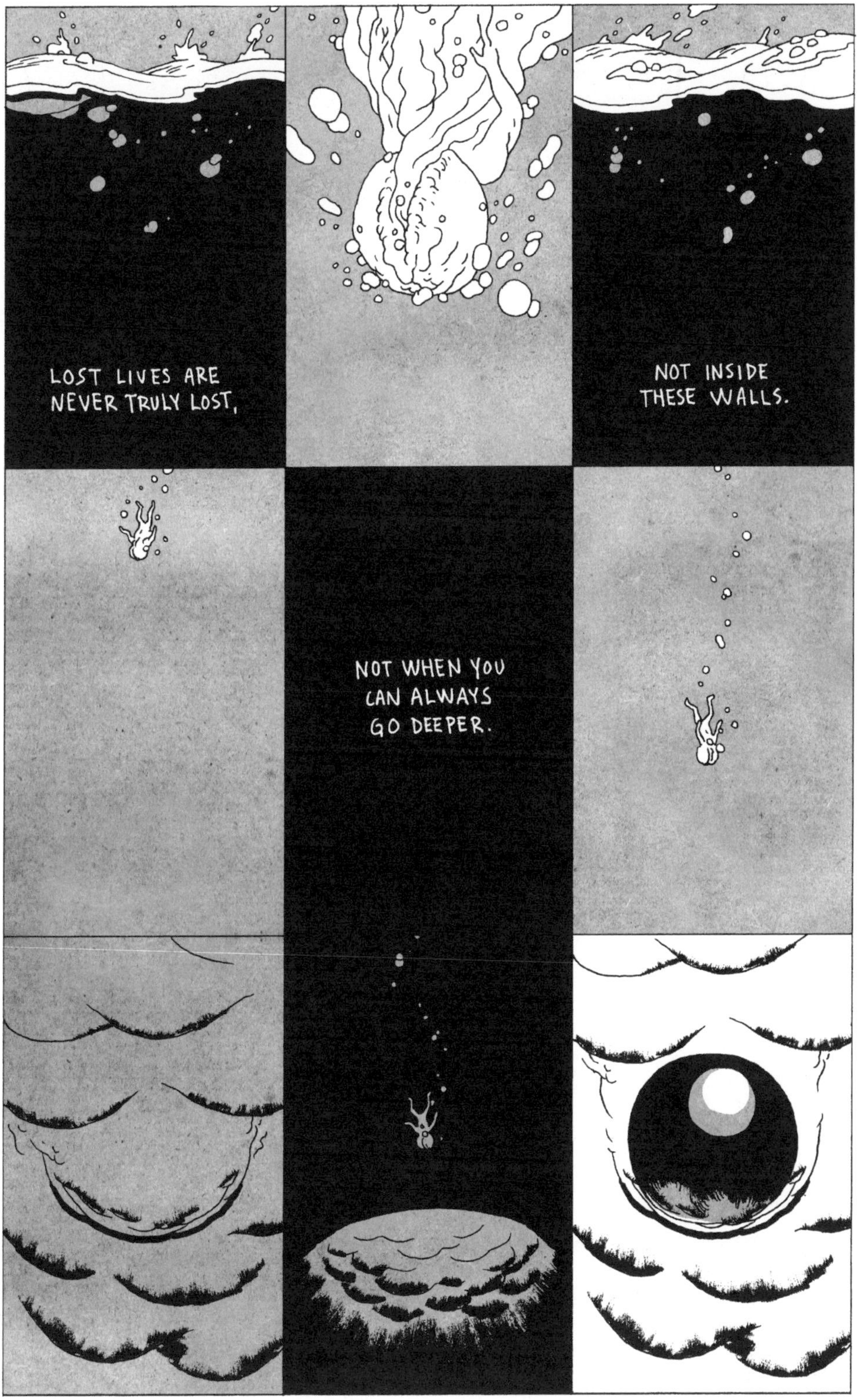
LOST LIVES ARE NEVER TRULY LOST,
NOT INSIDE THESE WALLS.
NOT WHEN YOU CAN ALWAYS GO DEEPER.

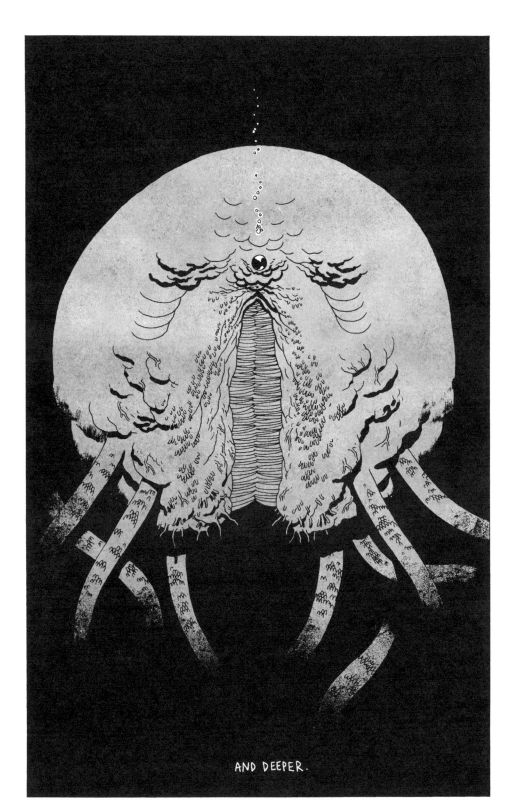

AND DEEPER.

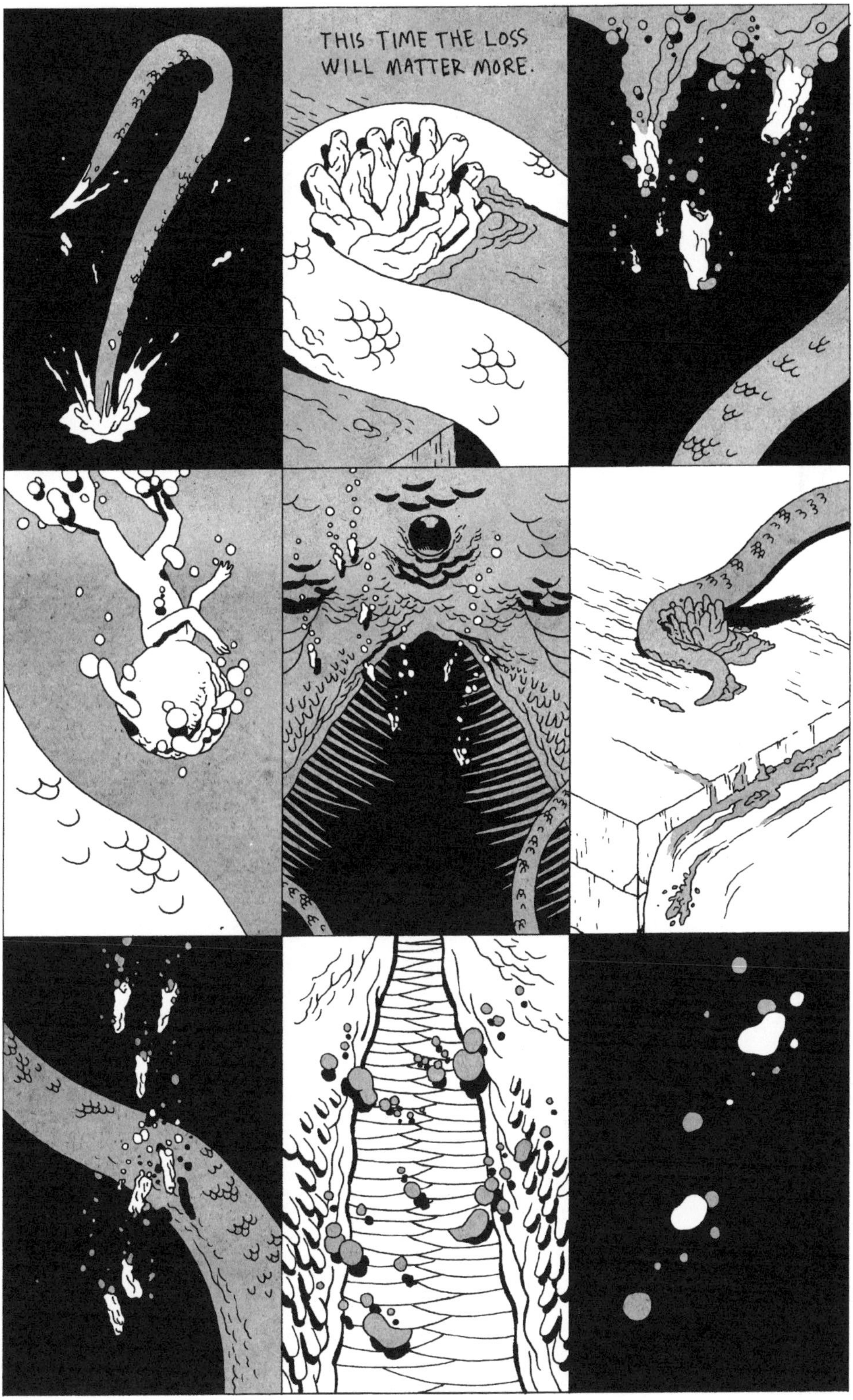
THIS TIME THE LOSS WILL MATTER MORE.

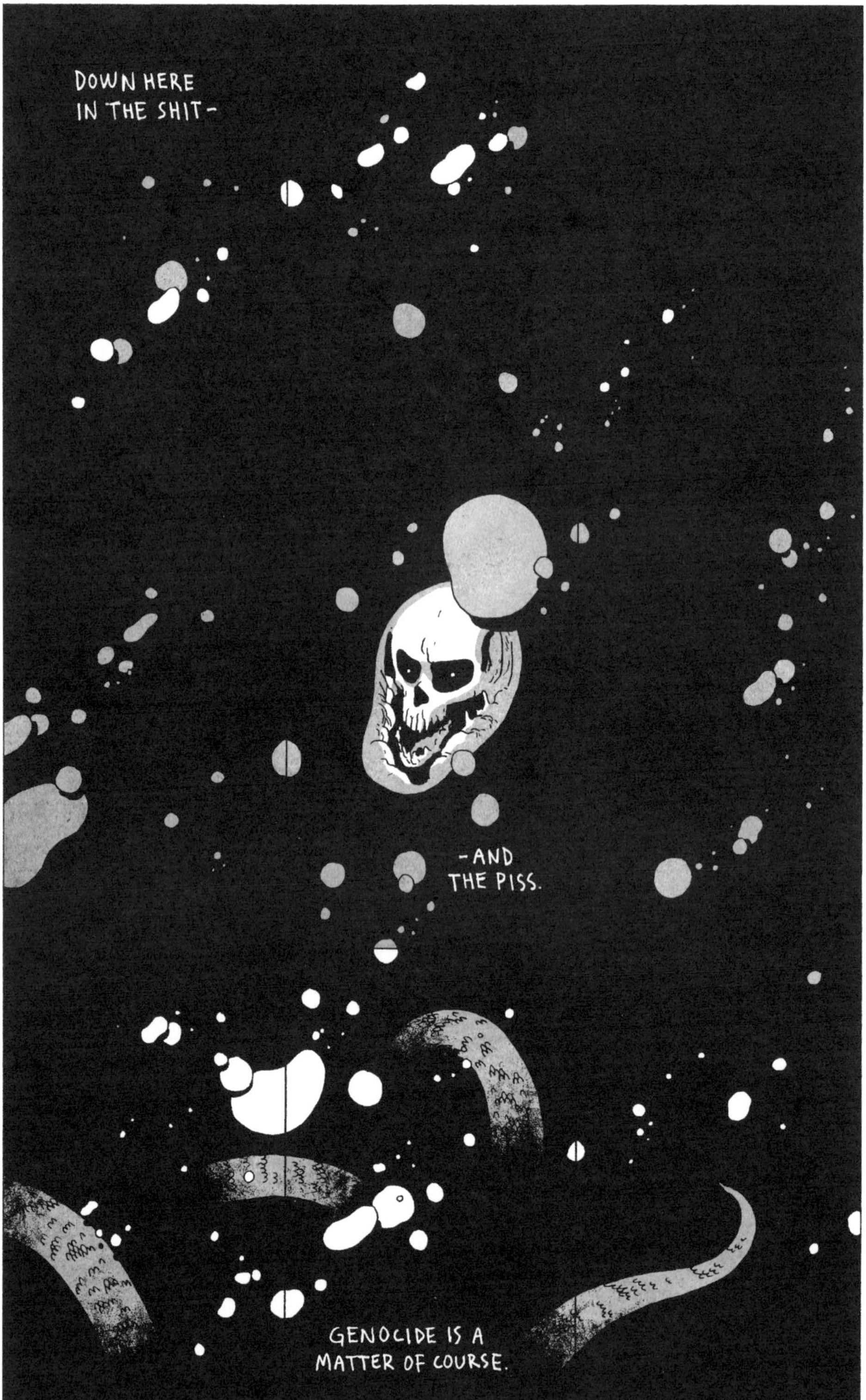
DOWN HERE
IN THE SHIT-
-AND
THE PISS.
GENOCIDE IS A
MATTER OF COURSE.

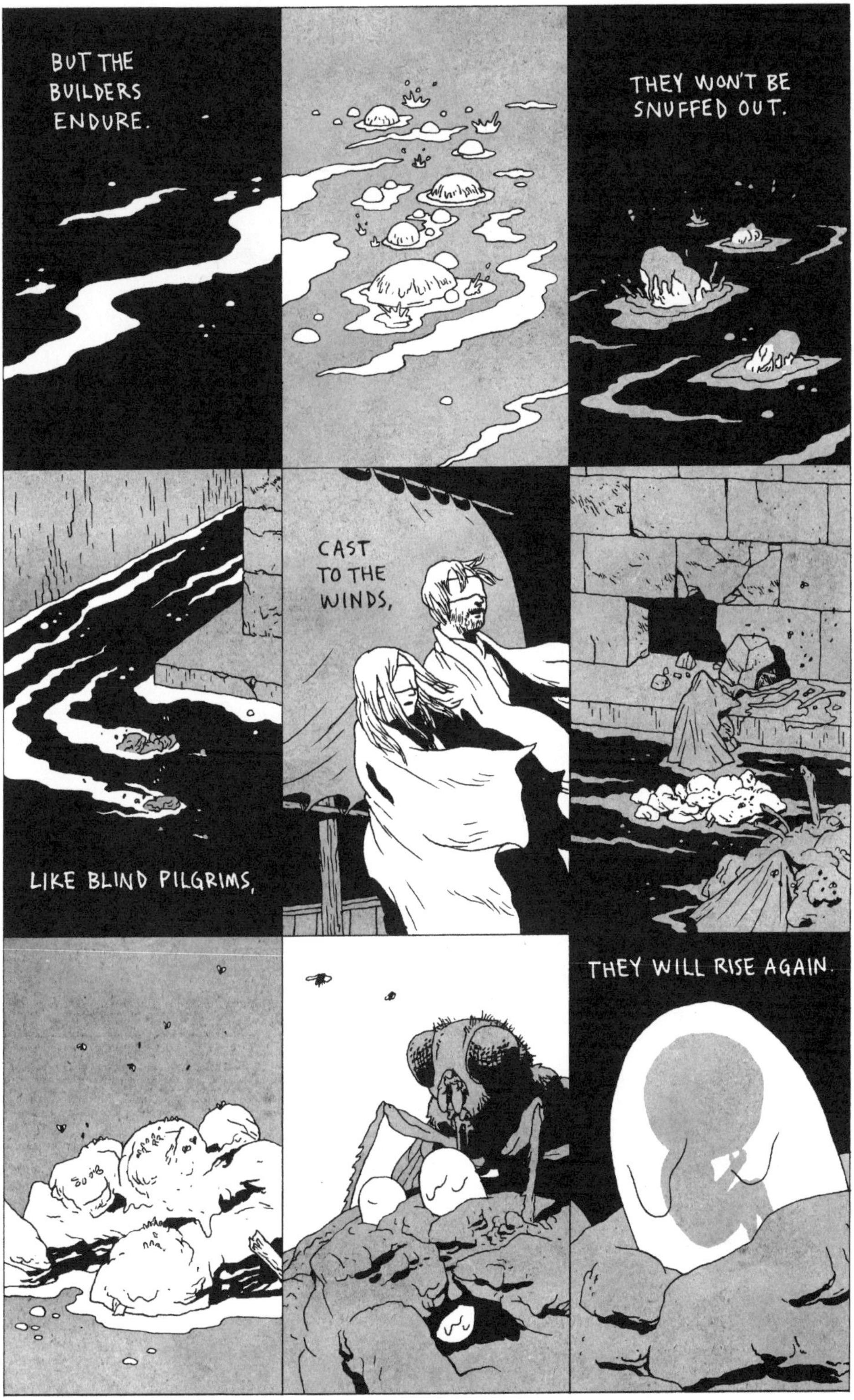
BUT THE BUILDERS ENDURE.
THEY WON'T BE SNUFFED OUT.
LIKE BLIND PILGRIMS,
CAST TO THE WINDS,
THEY WILL RISE AGAIN.

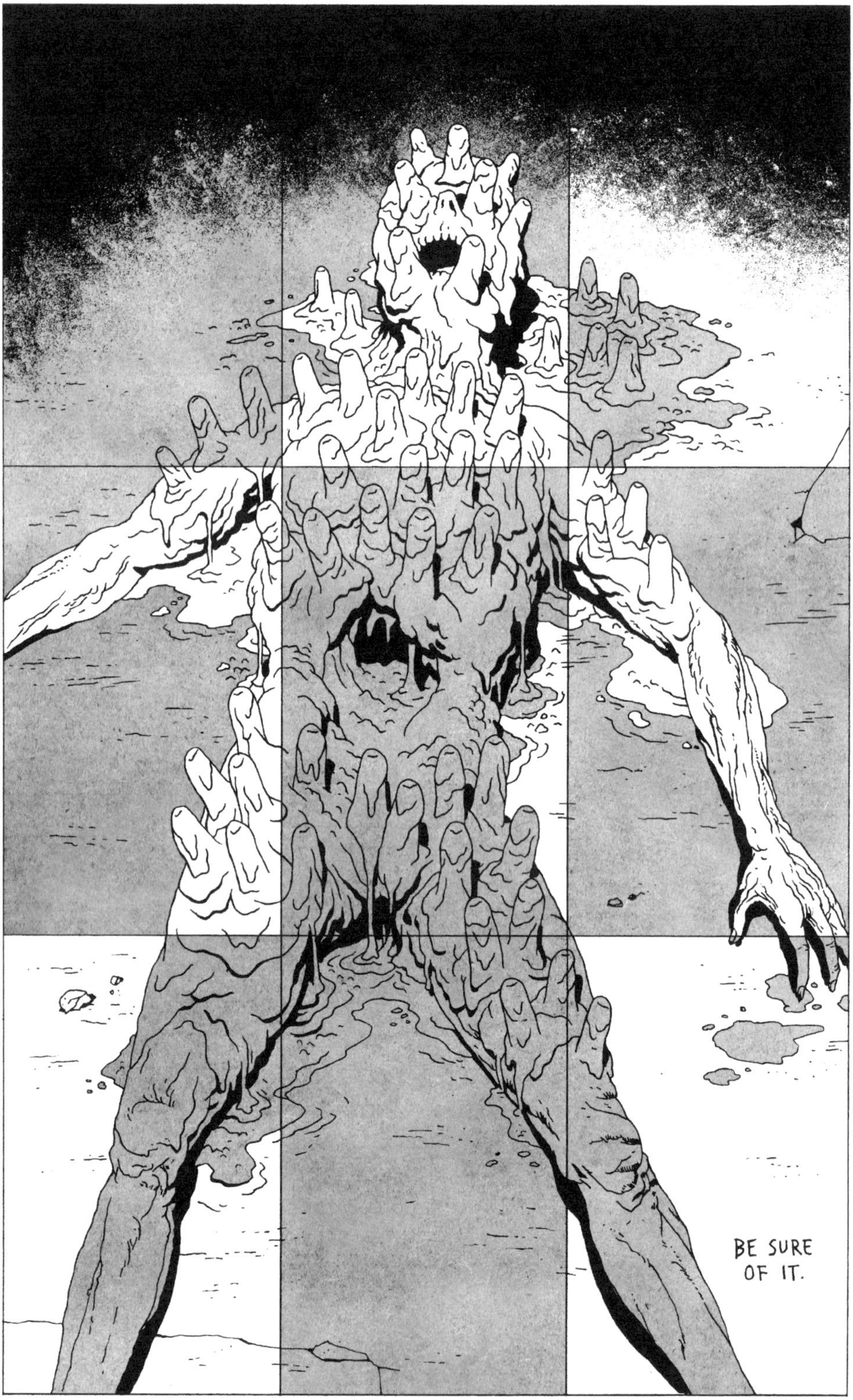
BE SURE OF IT.

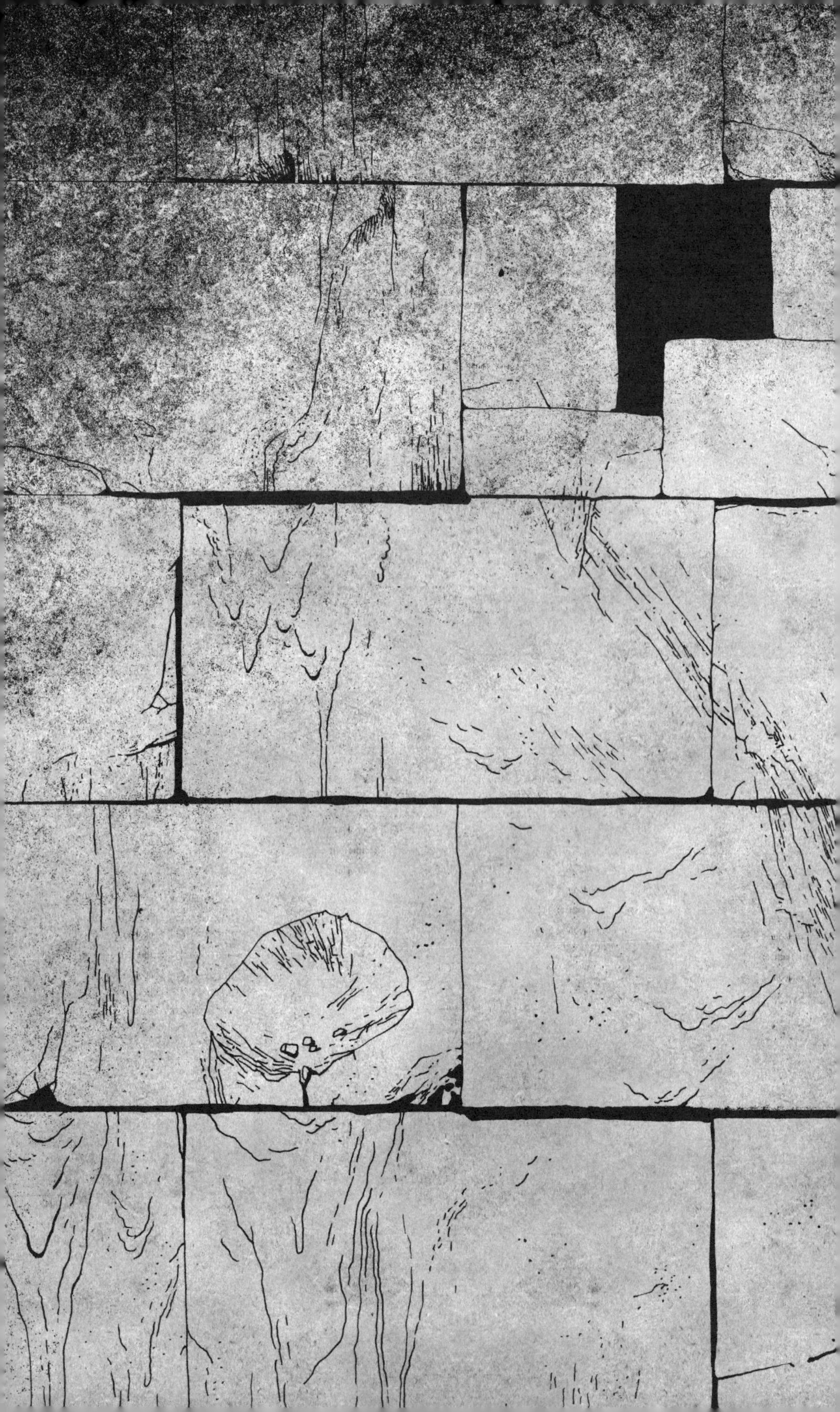

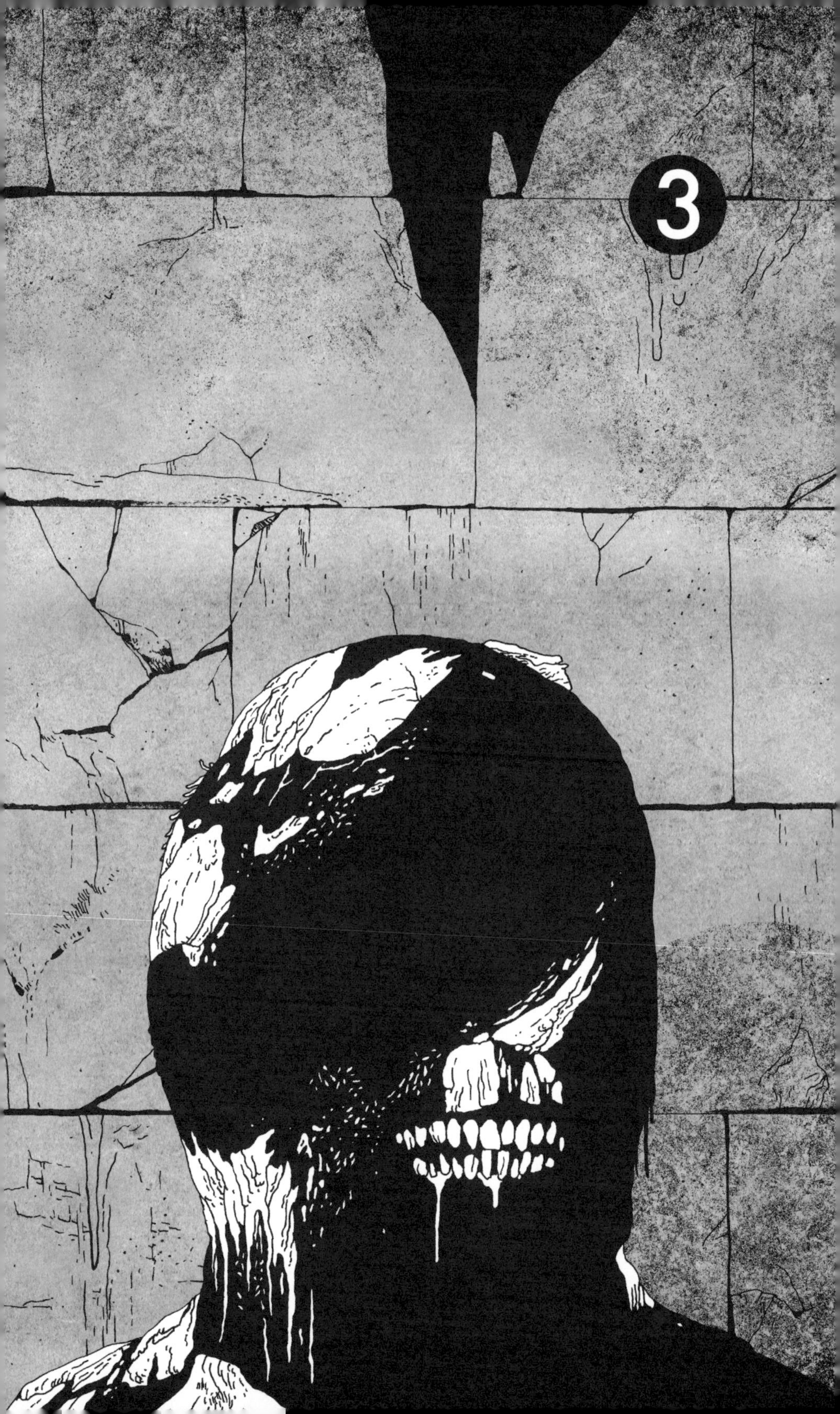
3

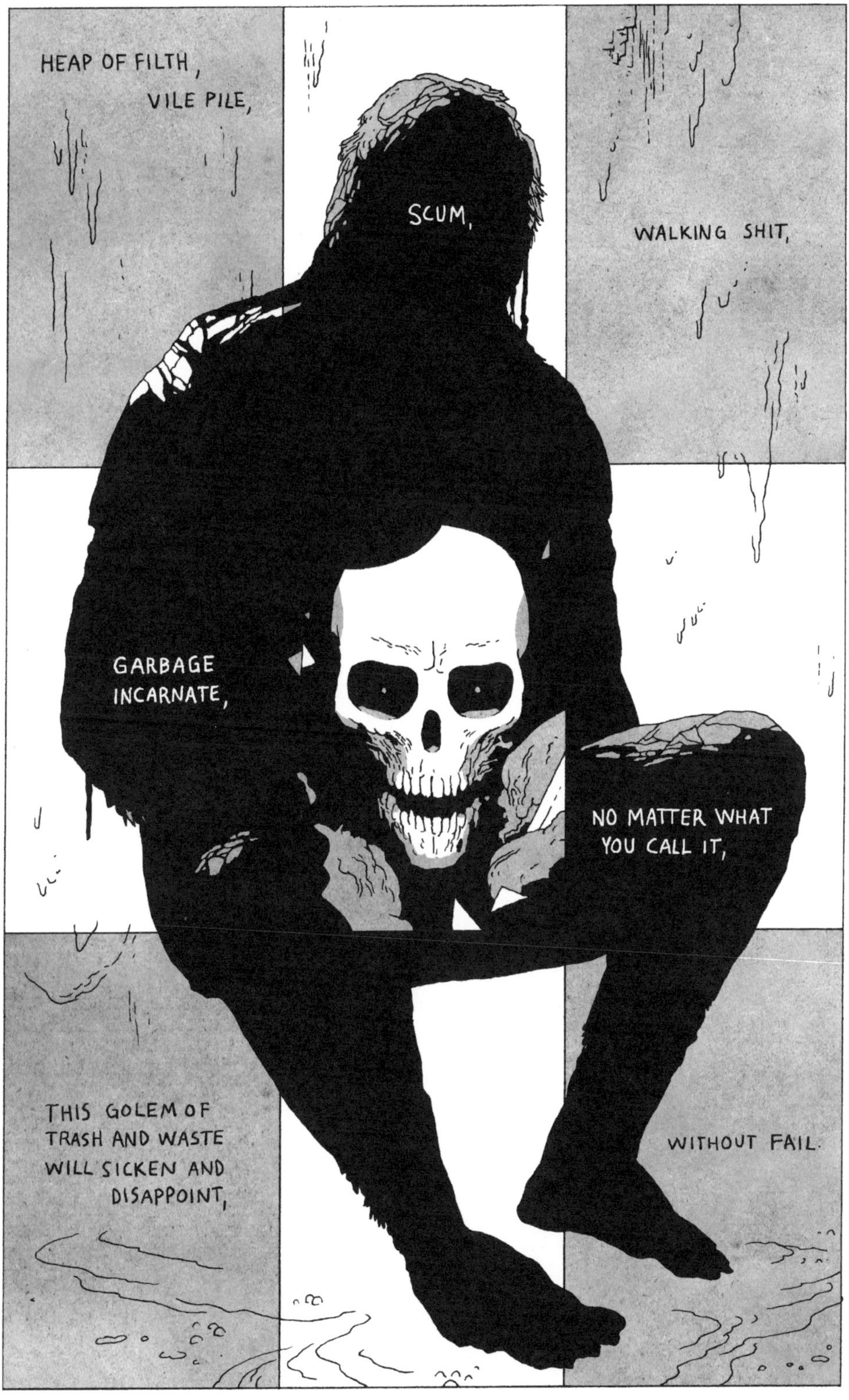
HEAP OF FILTH,
VILE PILE,
SCUM,
WALKING SHIT,
GARBAGE INCARNATE,
NO MATTER WHAT YOU CALL IT,
THIS GOLEM OF TRASH AND WASTE WILL SICKEN AND DISAPPOINT,
WITHOUT FAIL.

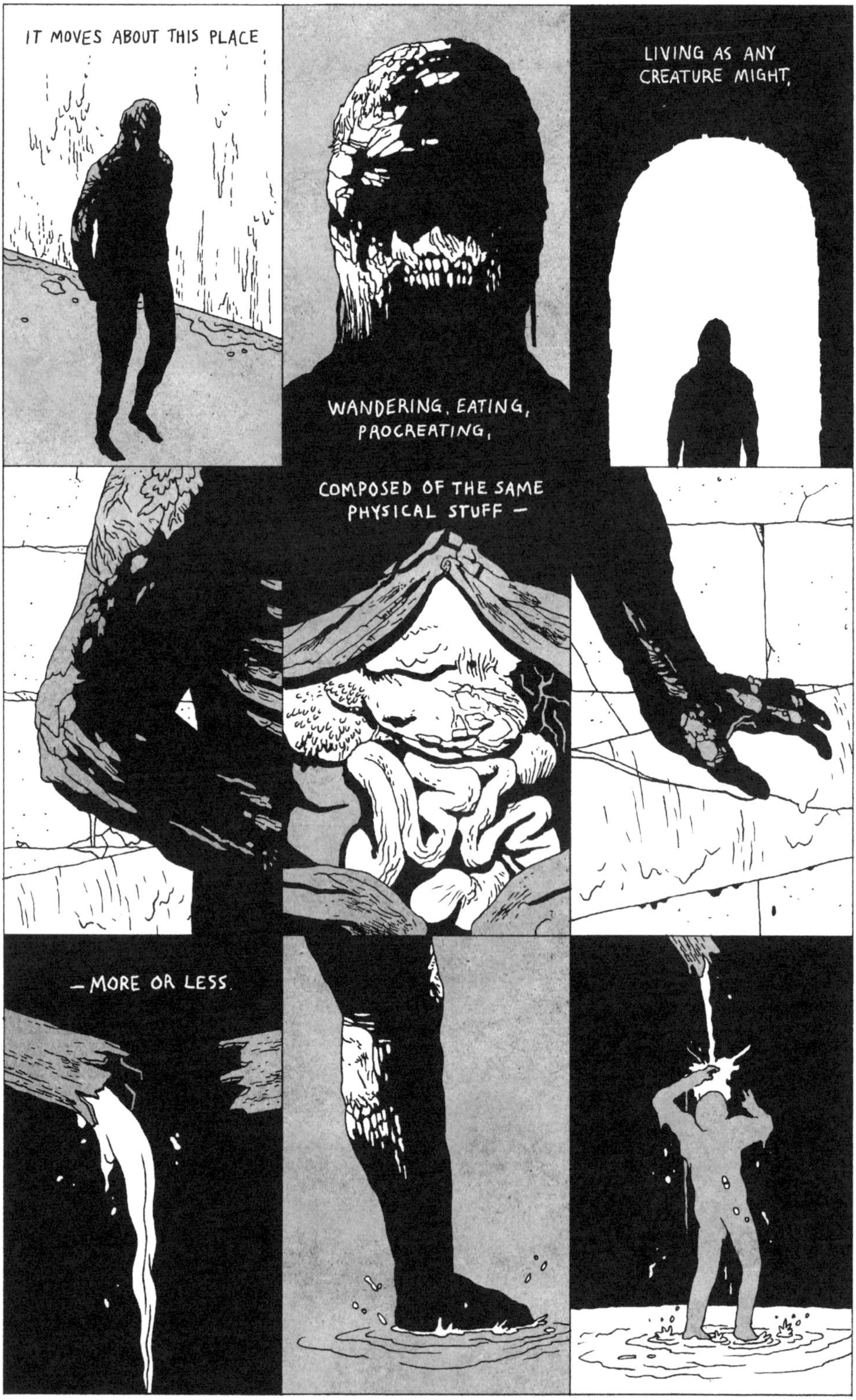
IT MOVES ABOUT THIS PLACE
WANDERING, EATING, PROCREATING,
LIVING AS ANY CREATURE MIGHT,
COMPOSED OF THE SAME PHYSICAL STUFF —
— MORE OR LESS.

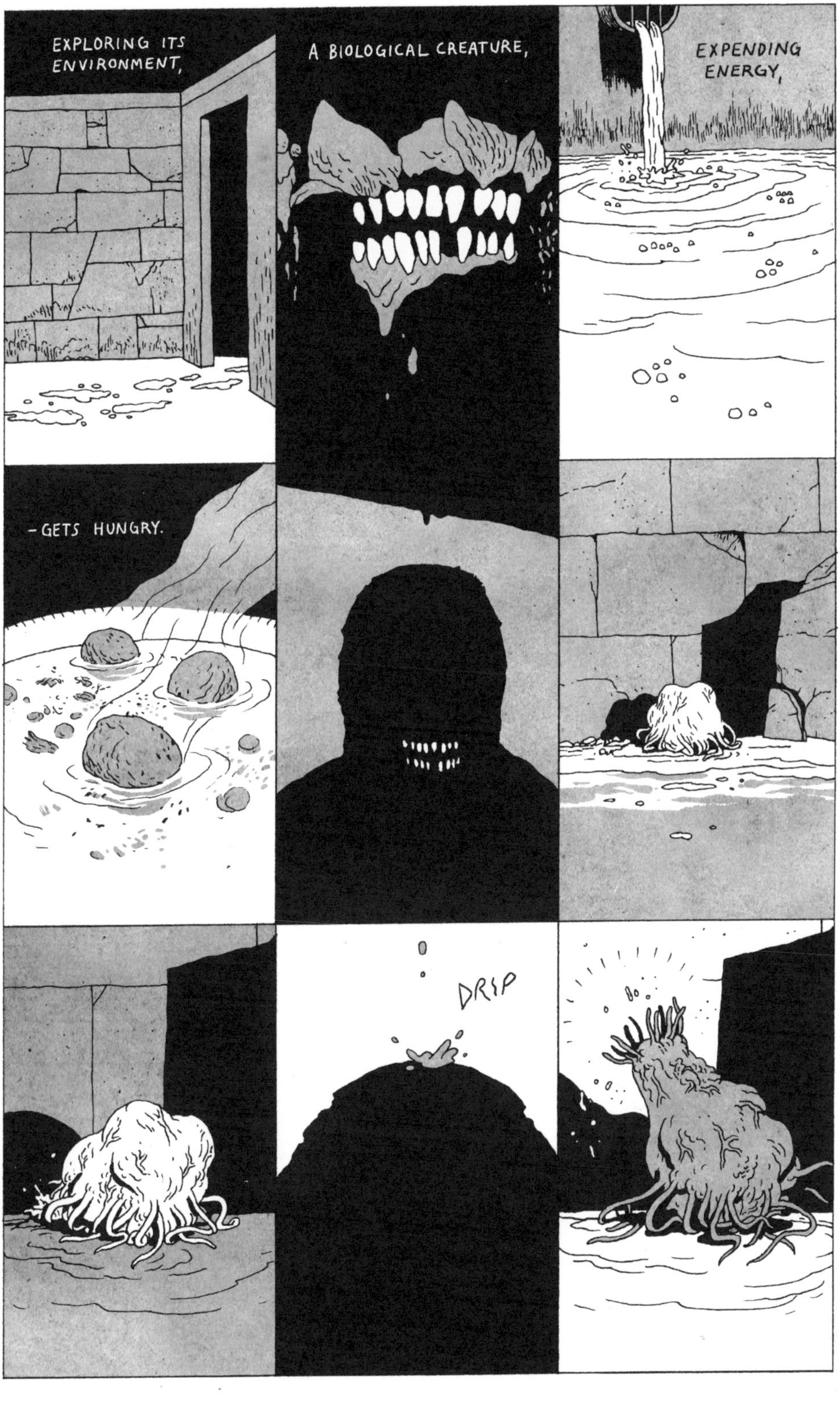
EXPLORING ITS ENVIRONMENT,
A BIOLOGICAL CREATURE,
EXPENDING ENERGY,
- GETS HUNGRY.
DRIP

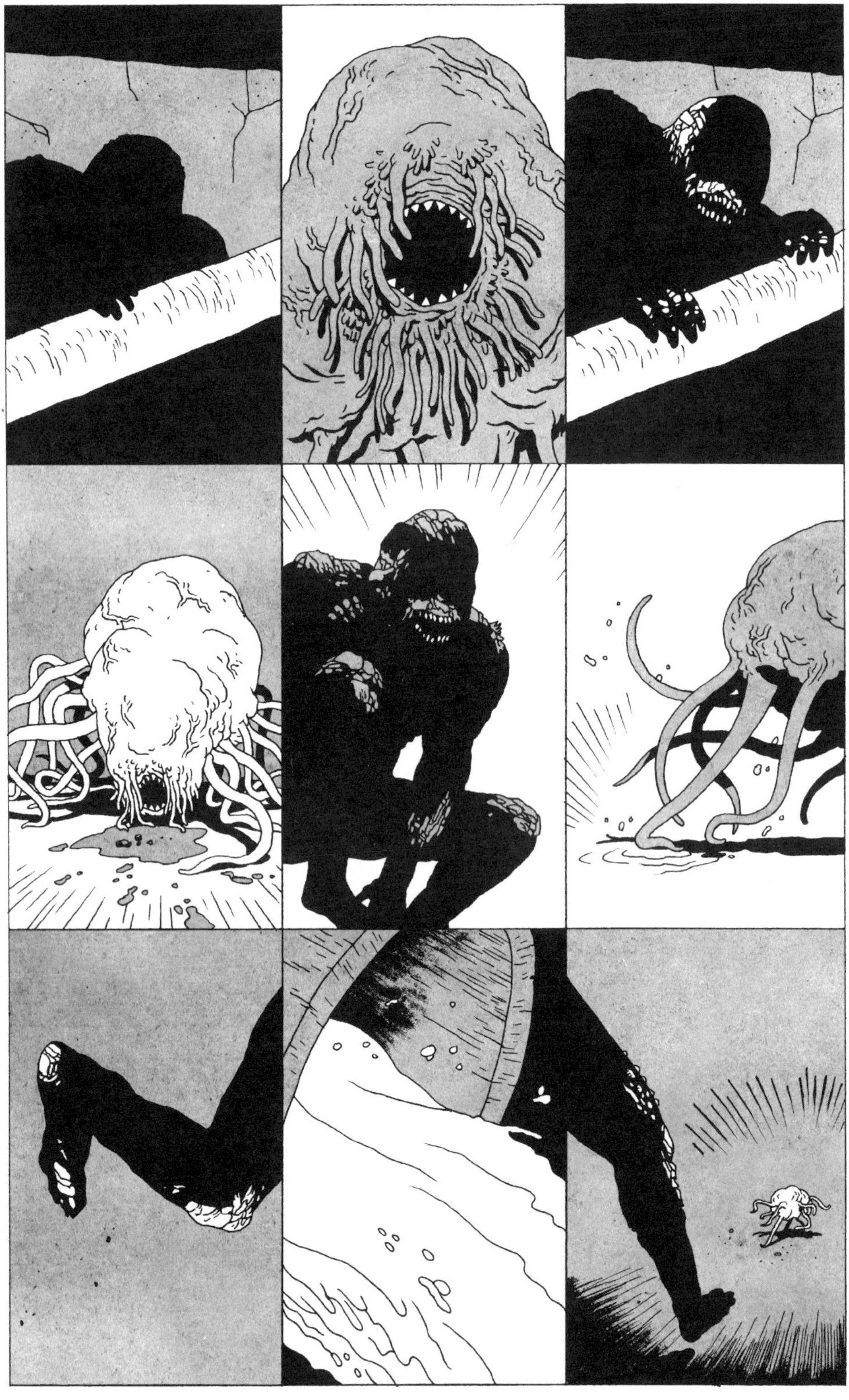

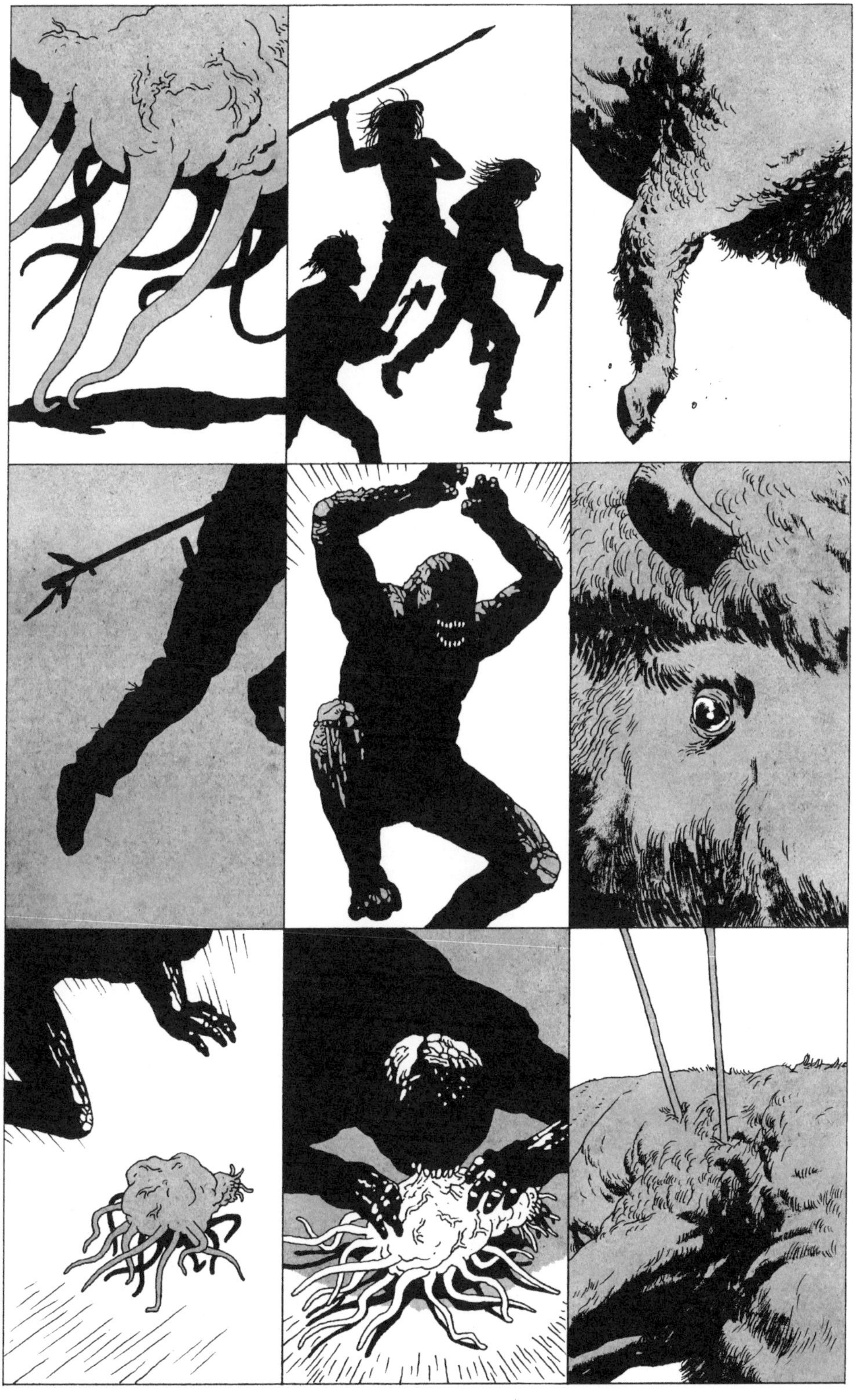

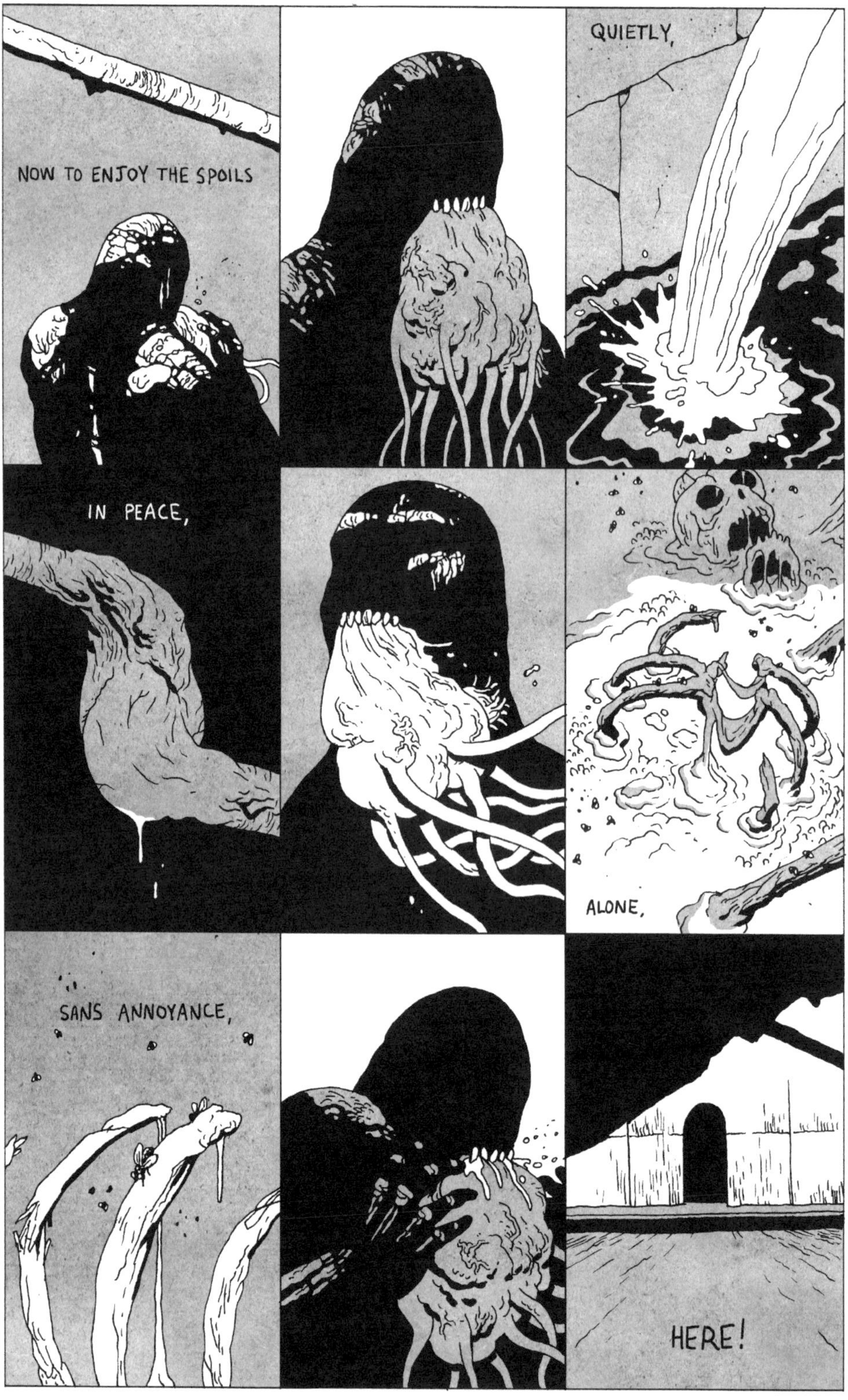
NOW TO ENJOY THE SPOILS
QUIETLY,
IN PEACE,
ALONE,
SANS ANNOYANCE,
HERE!

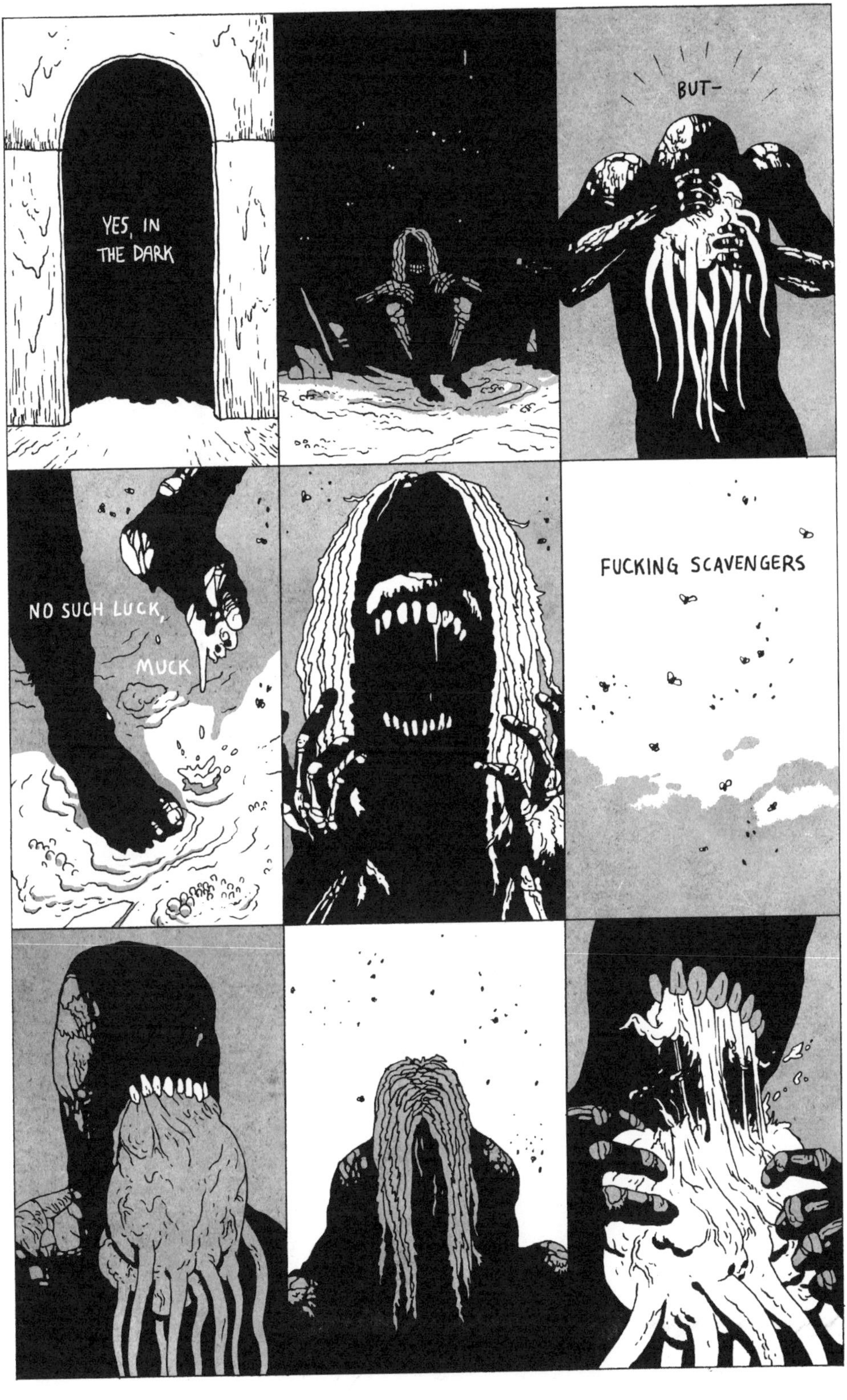
YES, IN THE DARK
BUT-
NO SUCH LUCK,
MUCK
FUCKING SCAVENGERS

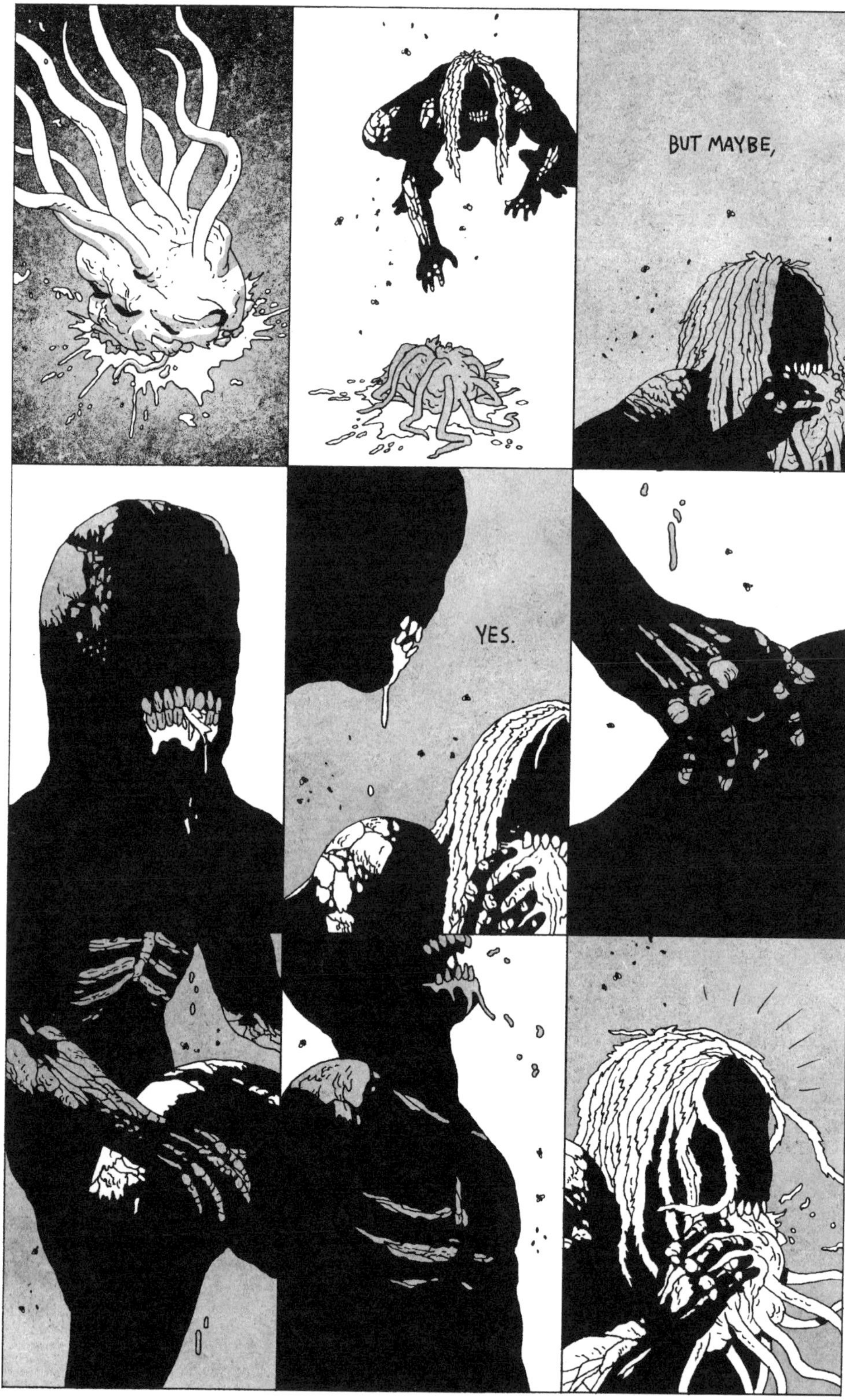
BUT MAYBE,
YES.

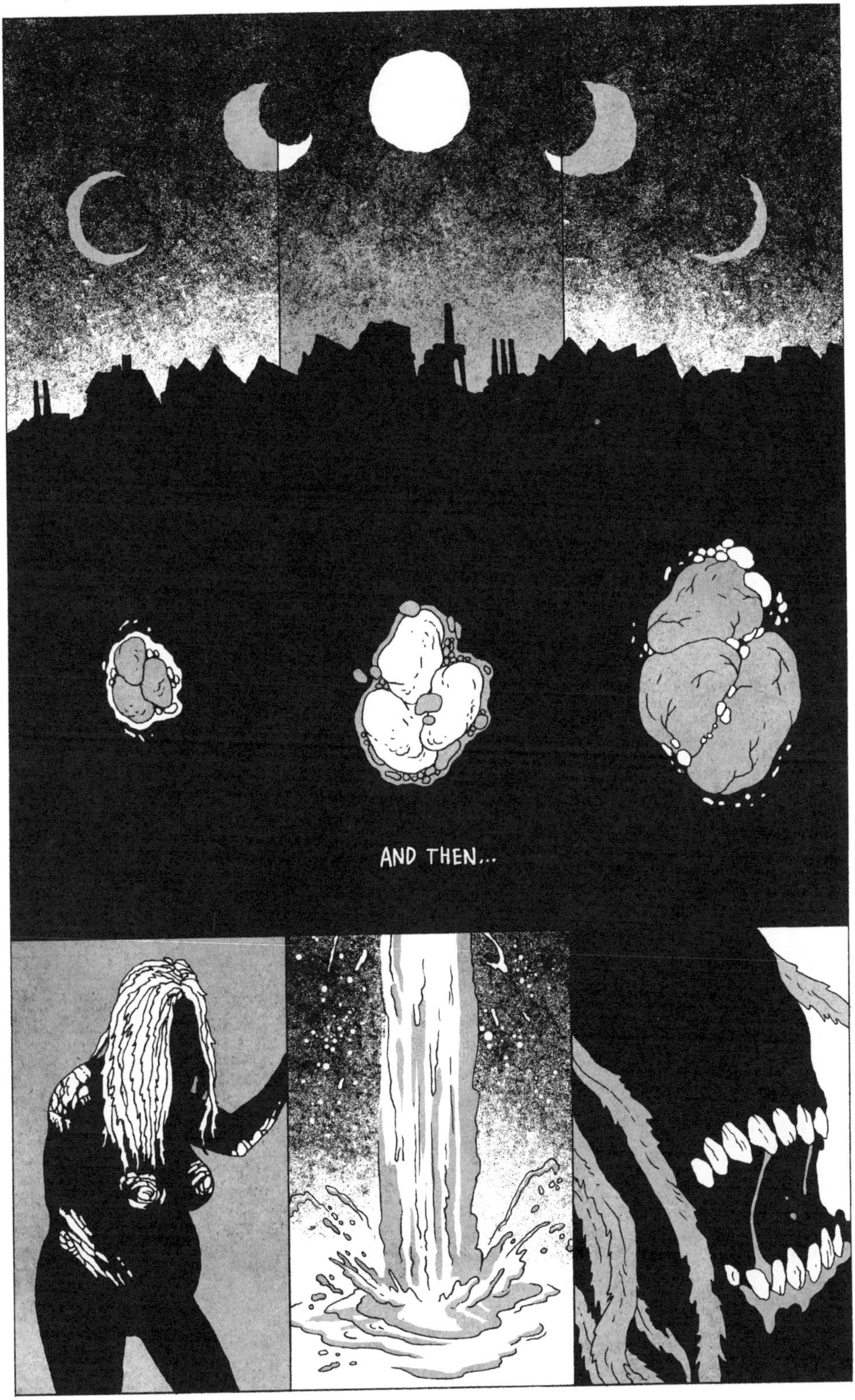
AND THEN...

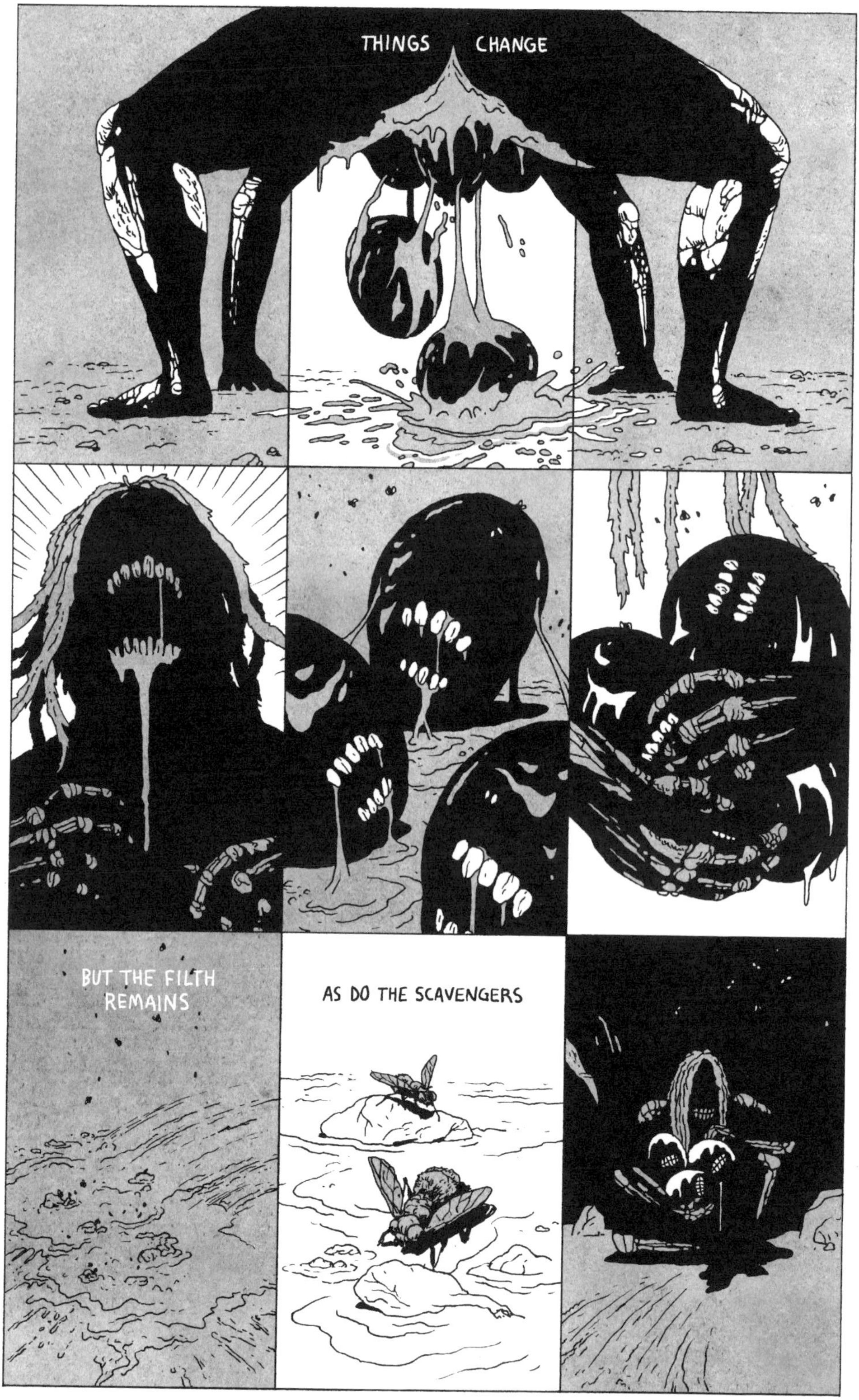
THINGS CHANGE
BUT THE FILTH REMAINS
AS DO THE SCAVENGERS

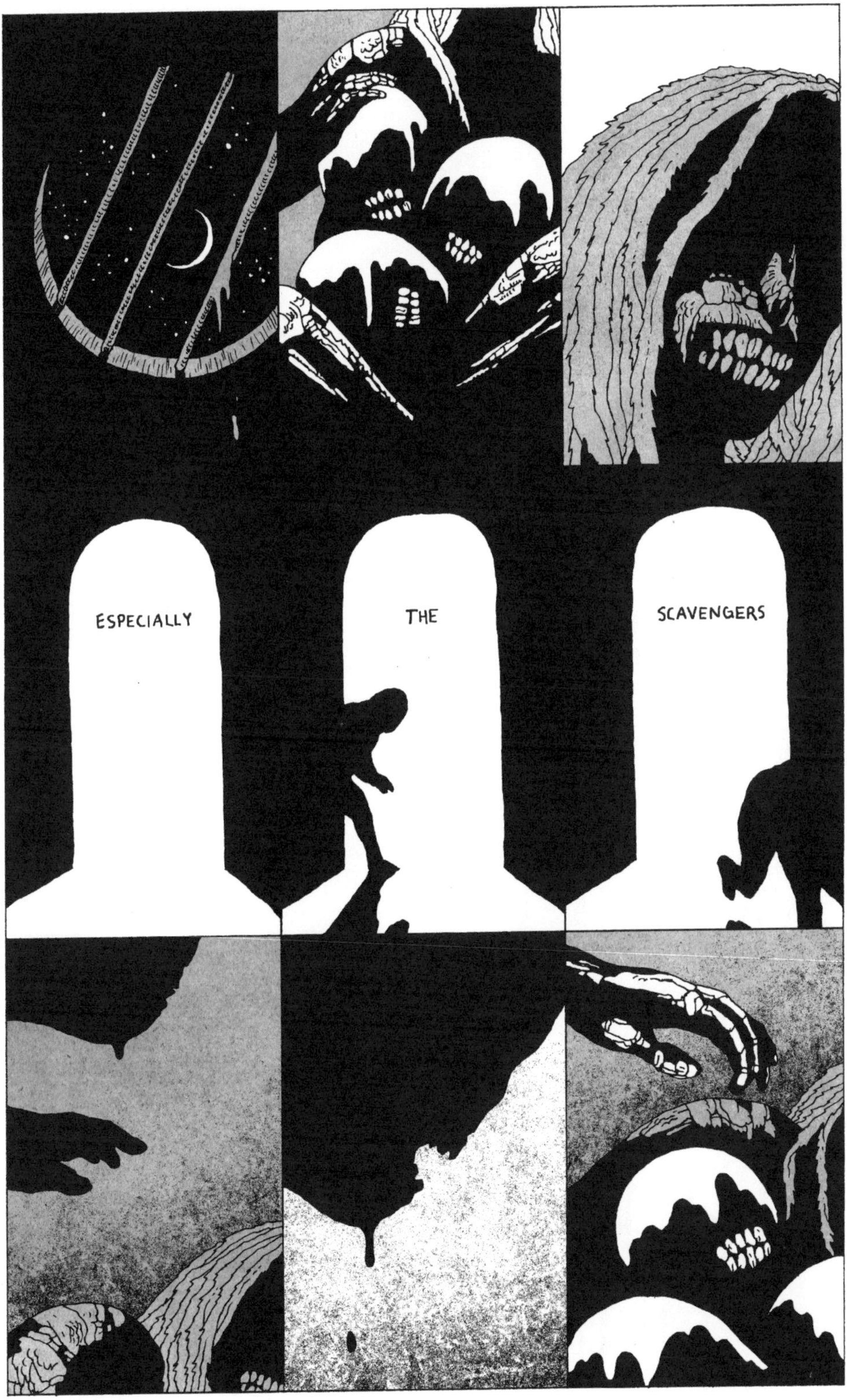
ESPECIALLY
THE
SCAVENGERS

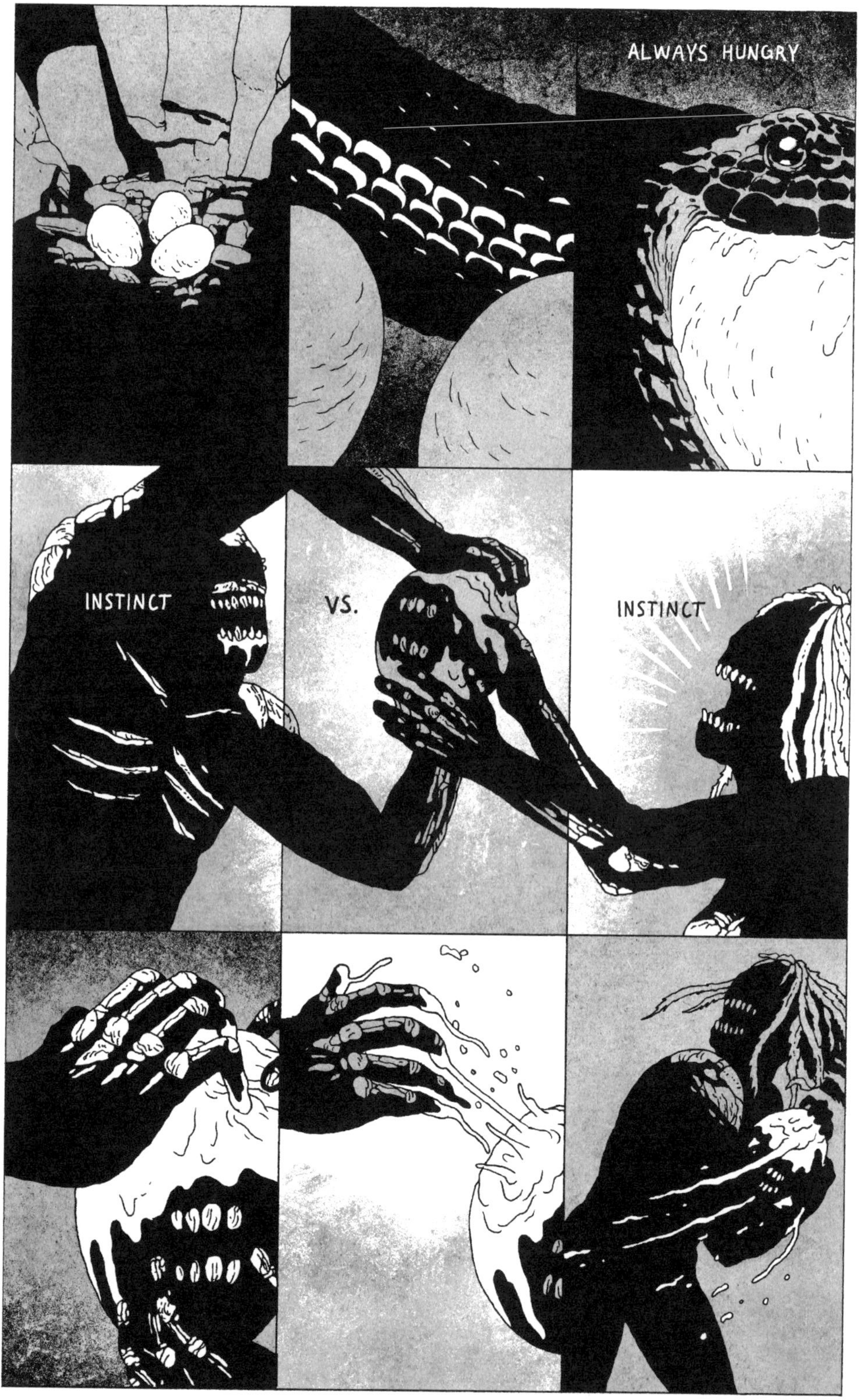
ALWAYS HUNGRY
INSTINCT
VS.
INSTINCT

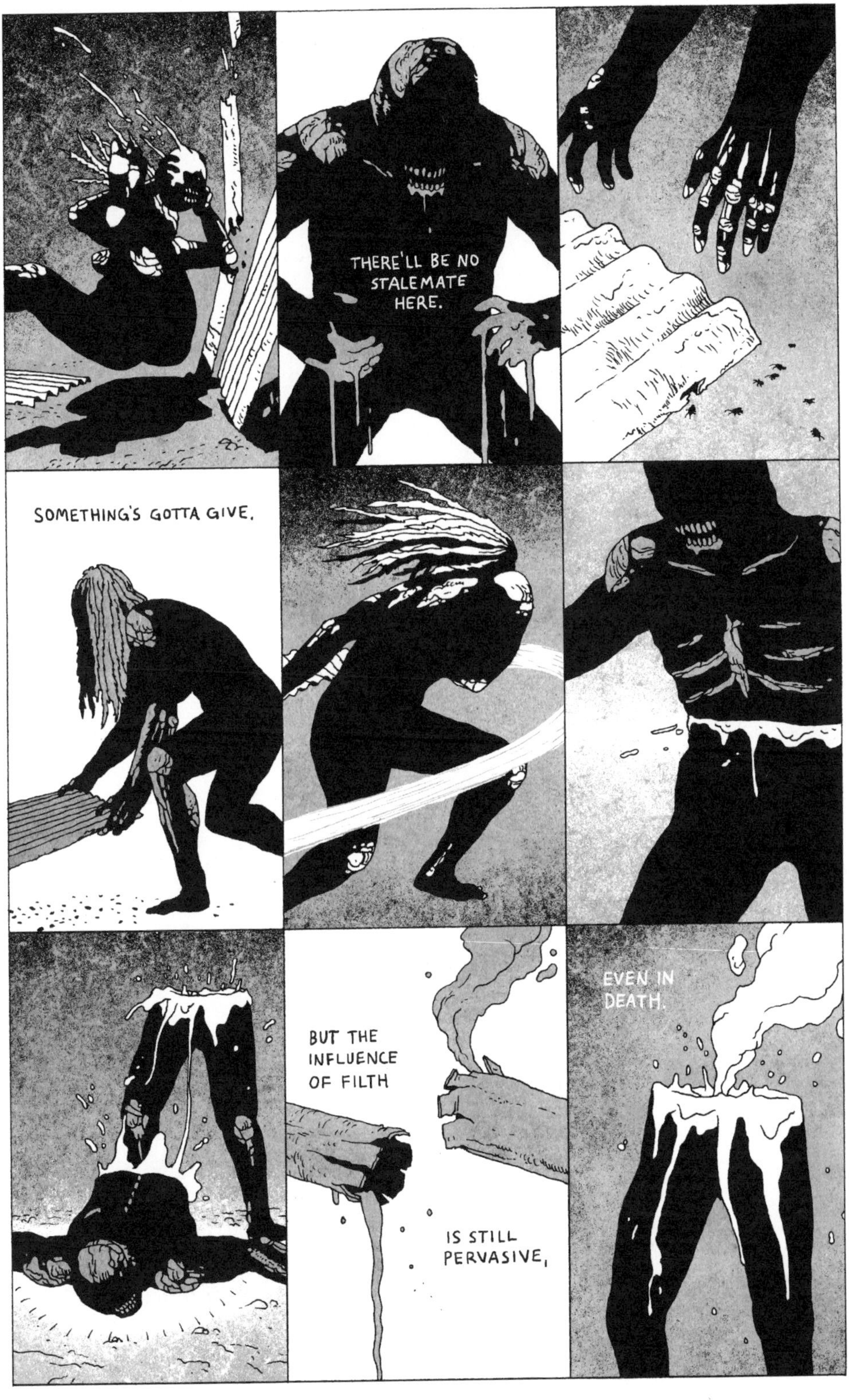
THERE'LL BE NO STALEMATE HERE.
SOMETHING'S GOTTA GIVE.
BUT THE INFLUENCE OF FILTH
IS STILL PERVASIVE,
EVEN IN DEATH.

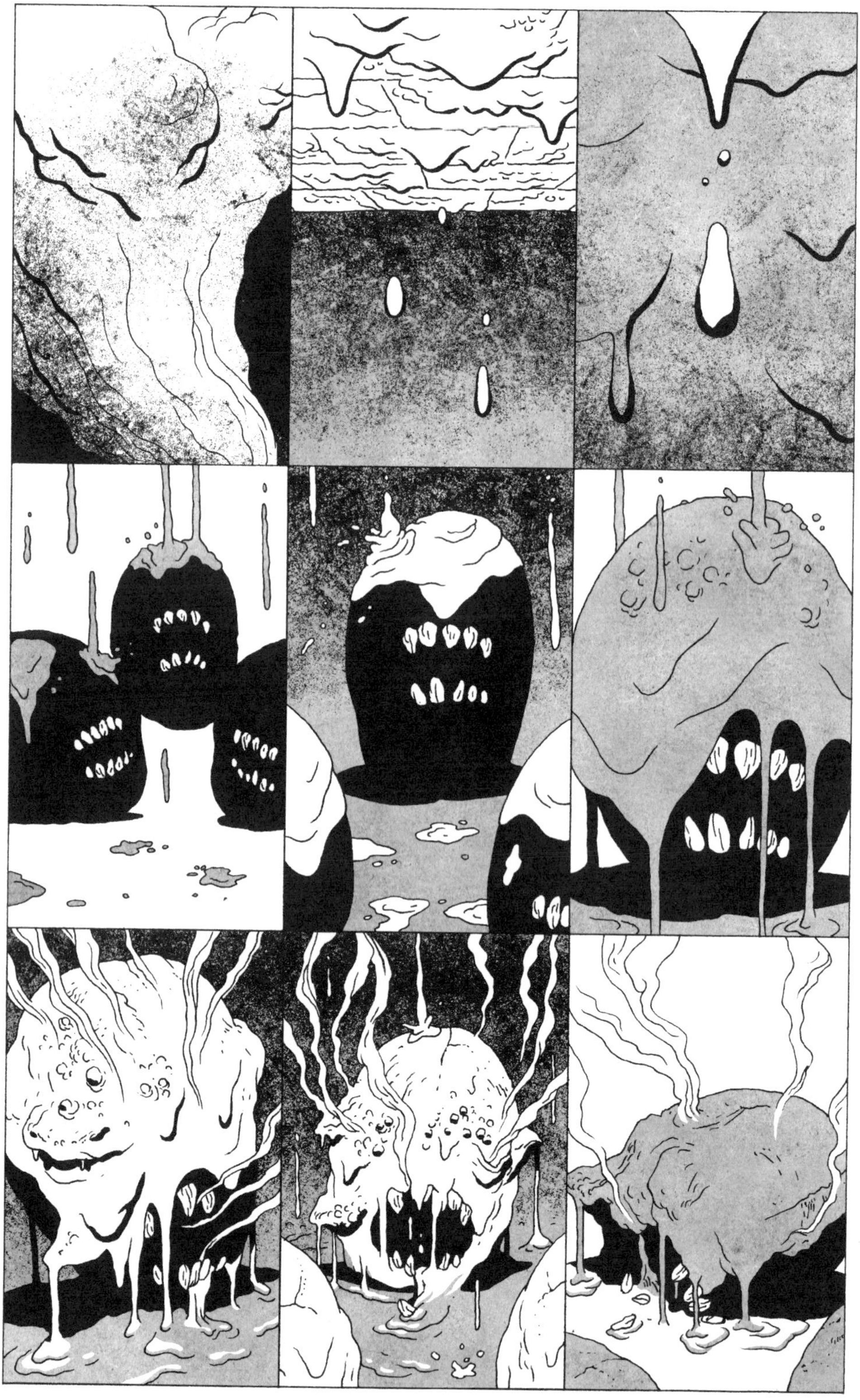

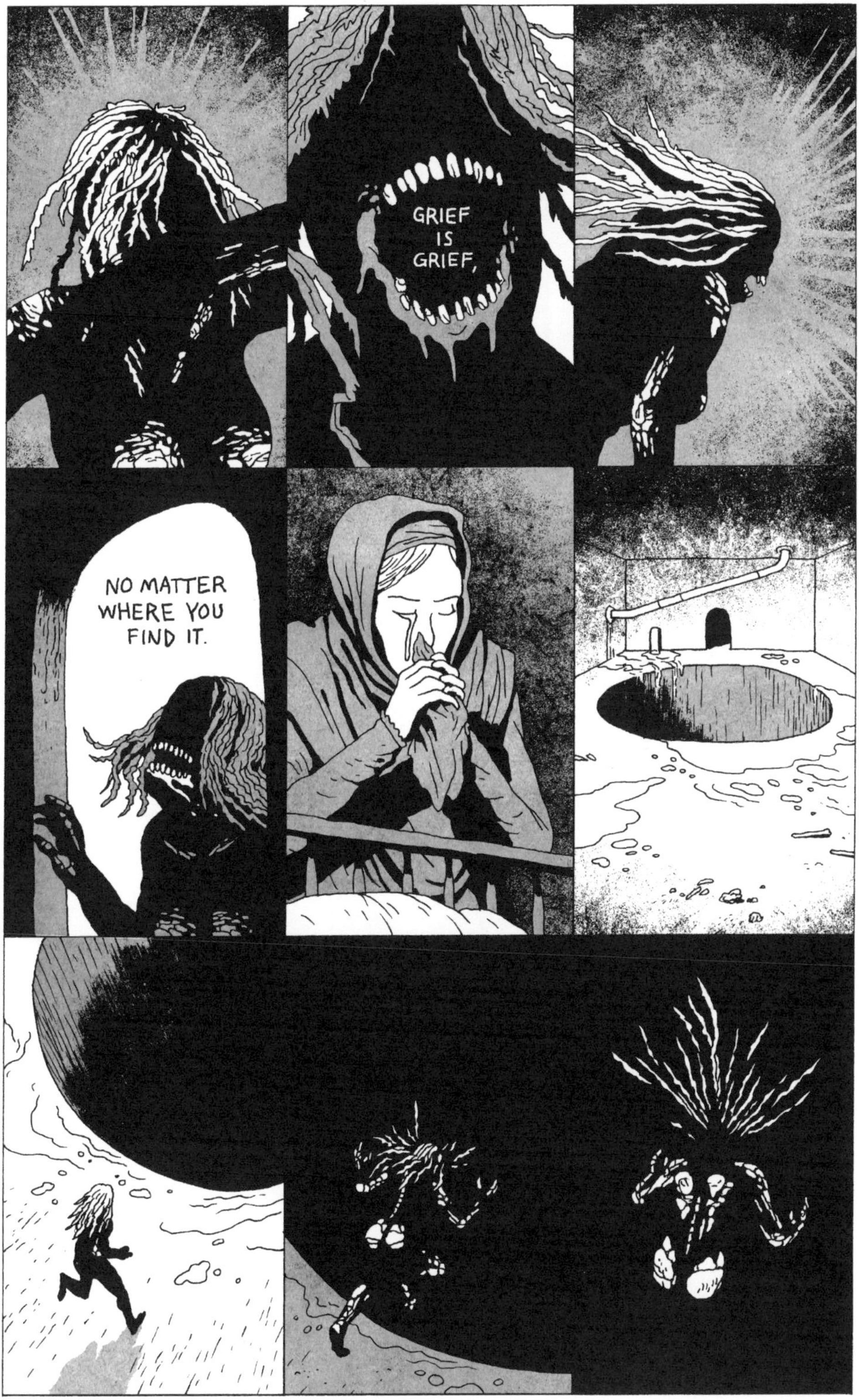
GRIEF IS GRIEF,
NO MATTER WHERE YOU FIND IT.

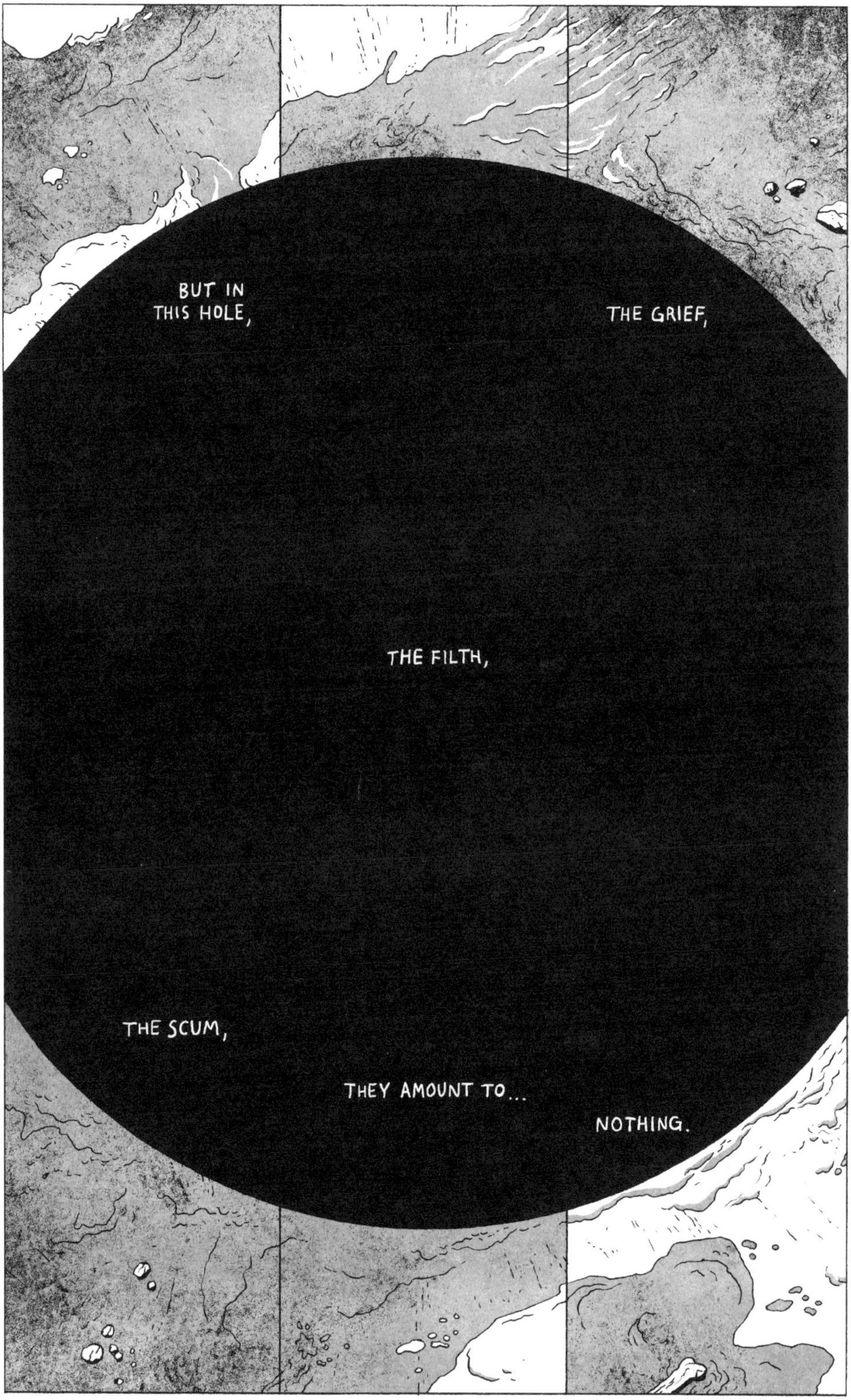
BUT IN THIS HOLE,
THE GRIEF,
THE FILTH,
THE SCUM,
THEY AMOUNT TO...
NOTHING.

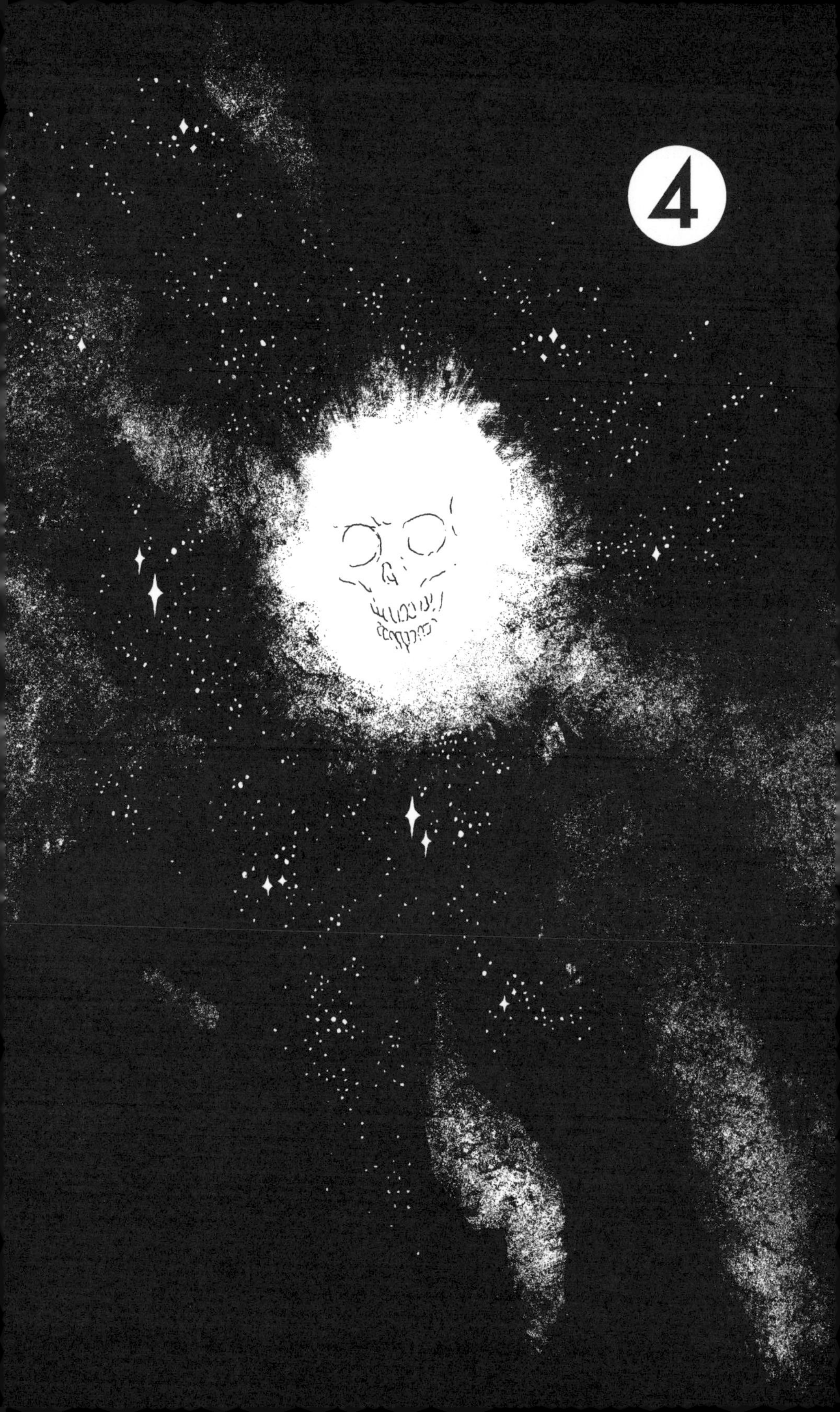
4

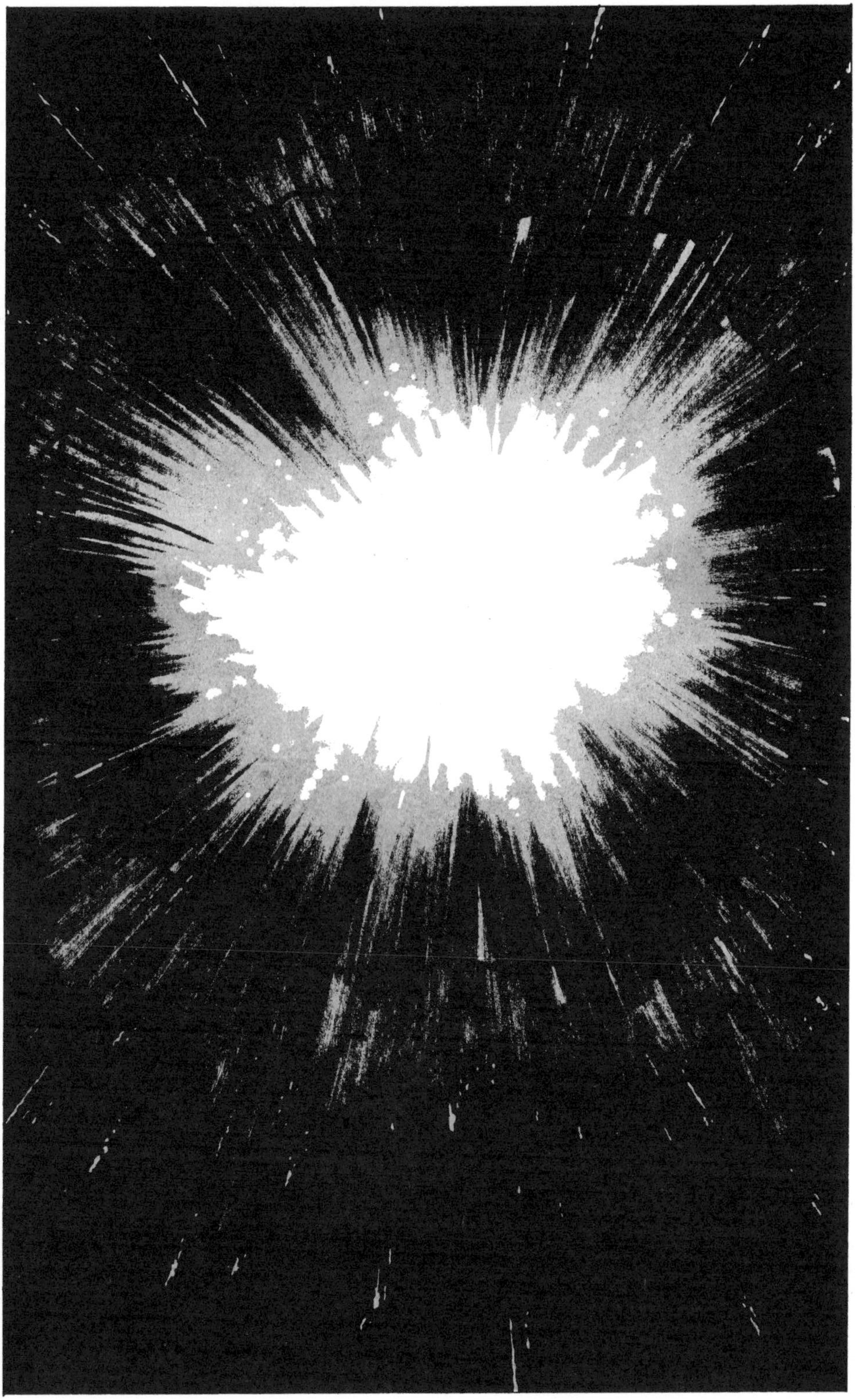

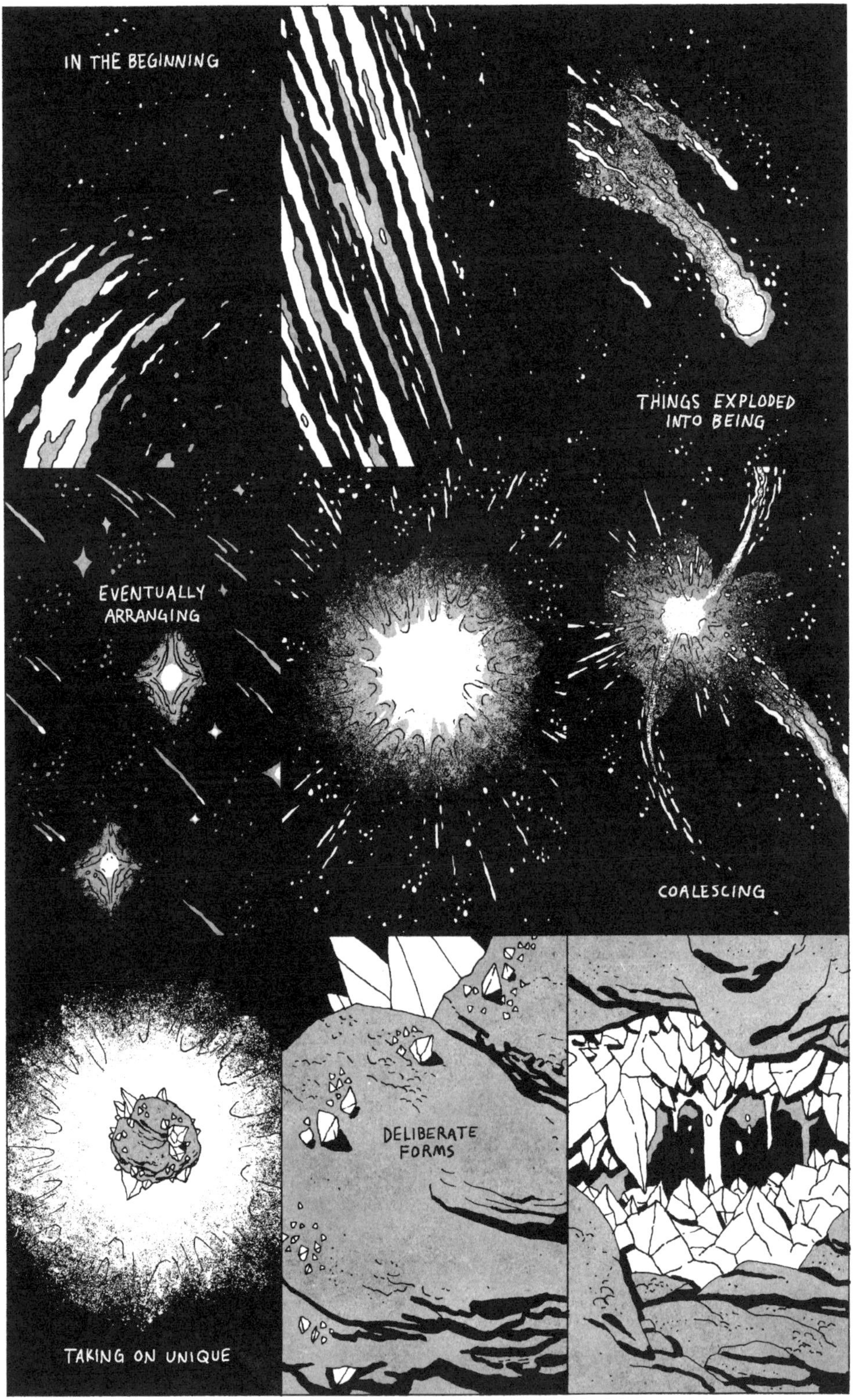
IN THE BEGINNING
THINGS EXPLODED INTO BEING
EVENTUALLY ARRANGING
COALESCING
TAKING ON UNIQUE
DELIBERATE FORMS

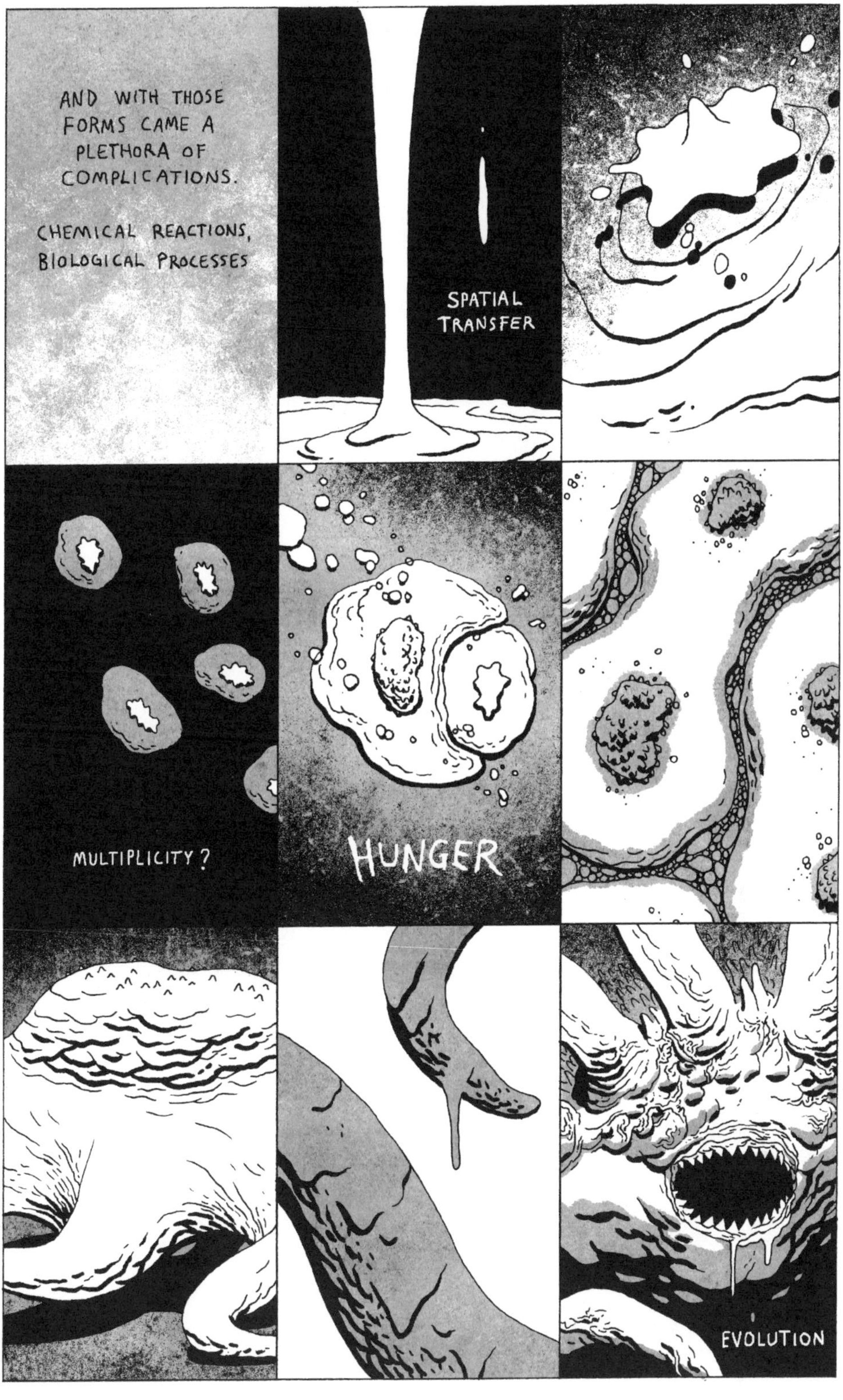
AND WITH THOSE FORMS CAME A PLETHORA OF COMPLICATIONS.
CHEMICAL REACTIONS, BIOLOGICAL PROCESSES
SPATIAL TRANSFER
MULTIPLICITY?
HUNGER
EVOLUTION

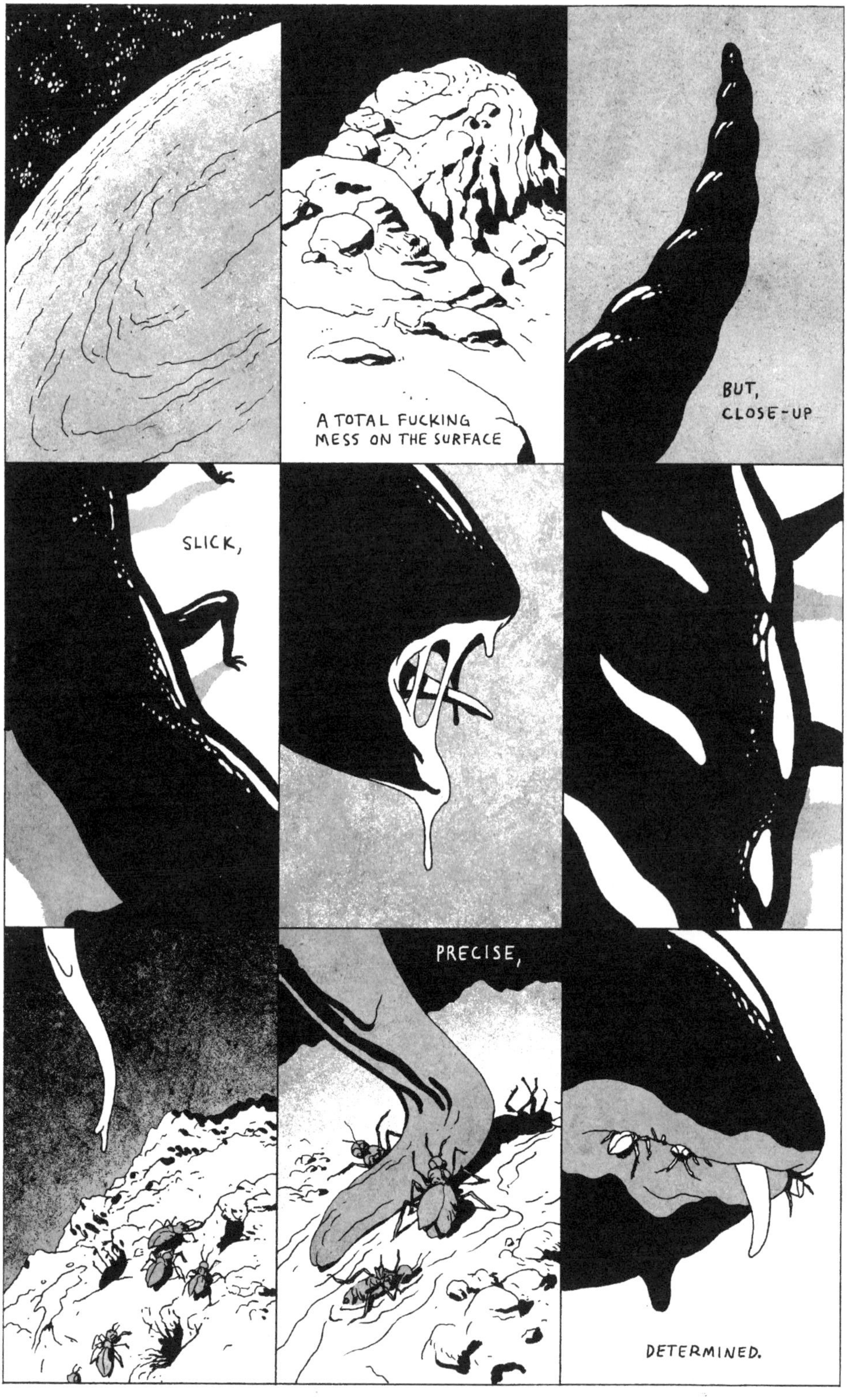
A TOTAL FUCKING
MESS ON THE SURFACE
BUT,
CLOSE-UP
SLICK,
PRECISE,
DETERMINED.

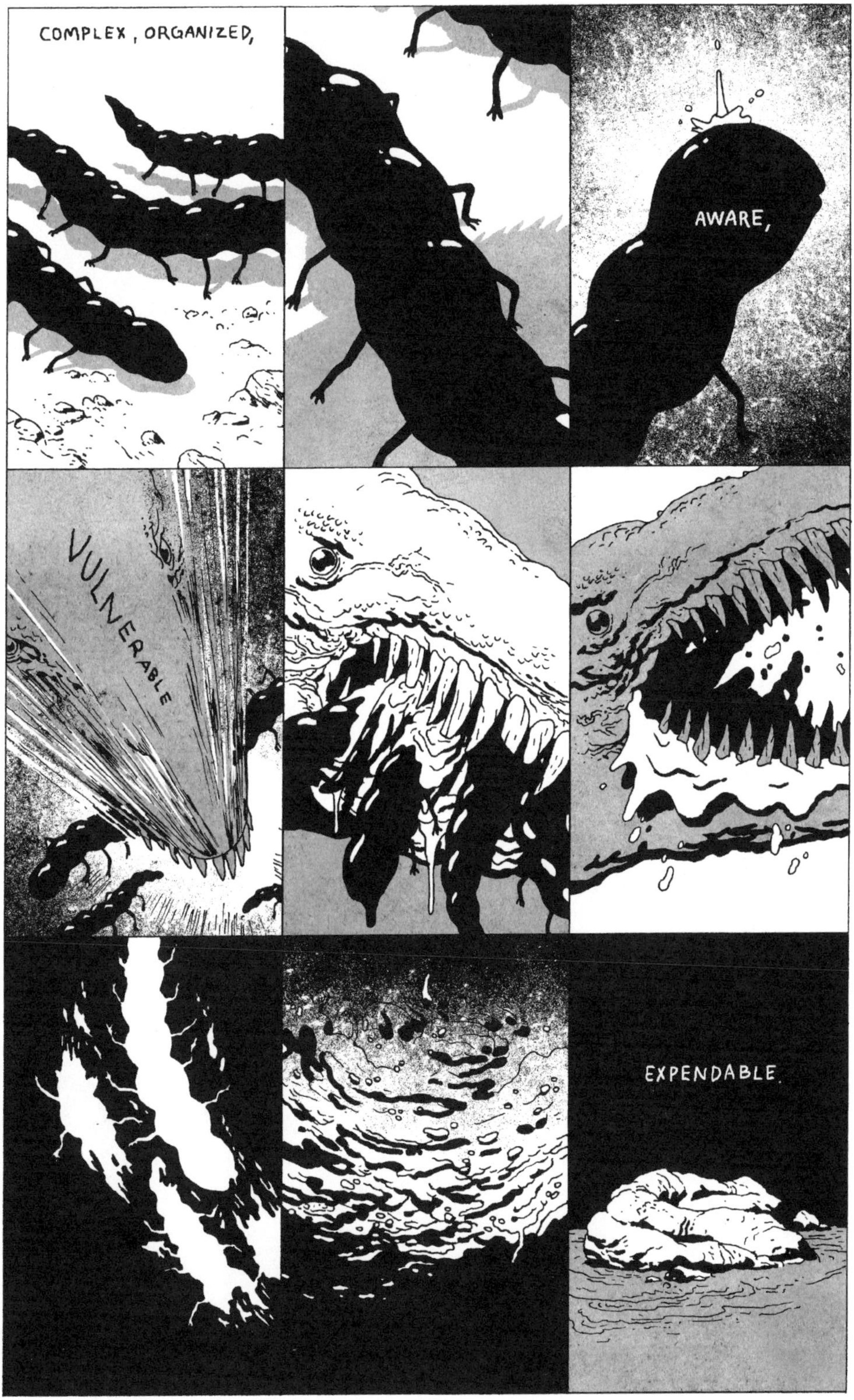
COMPLEX, ORGANIZED,
AWARE,
VULNERABLE
EXPENDABLE.

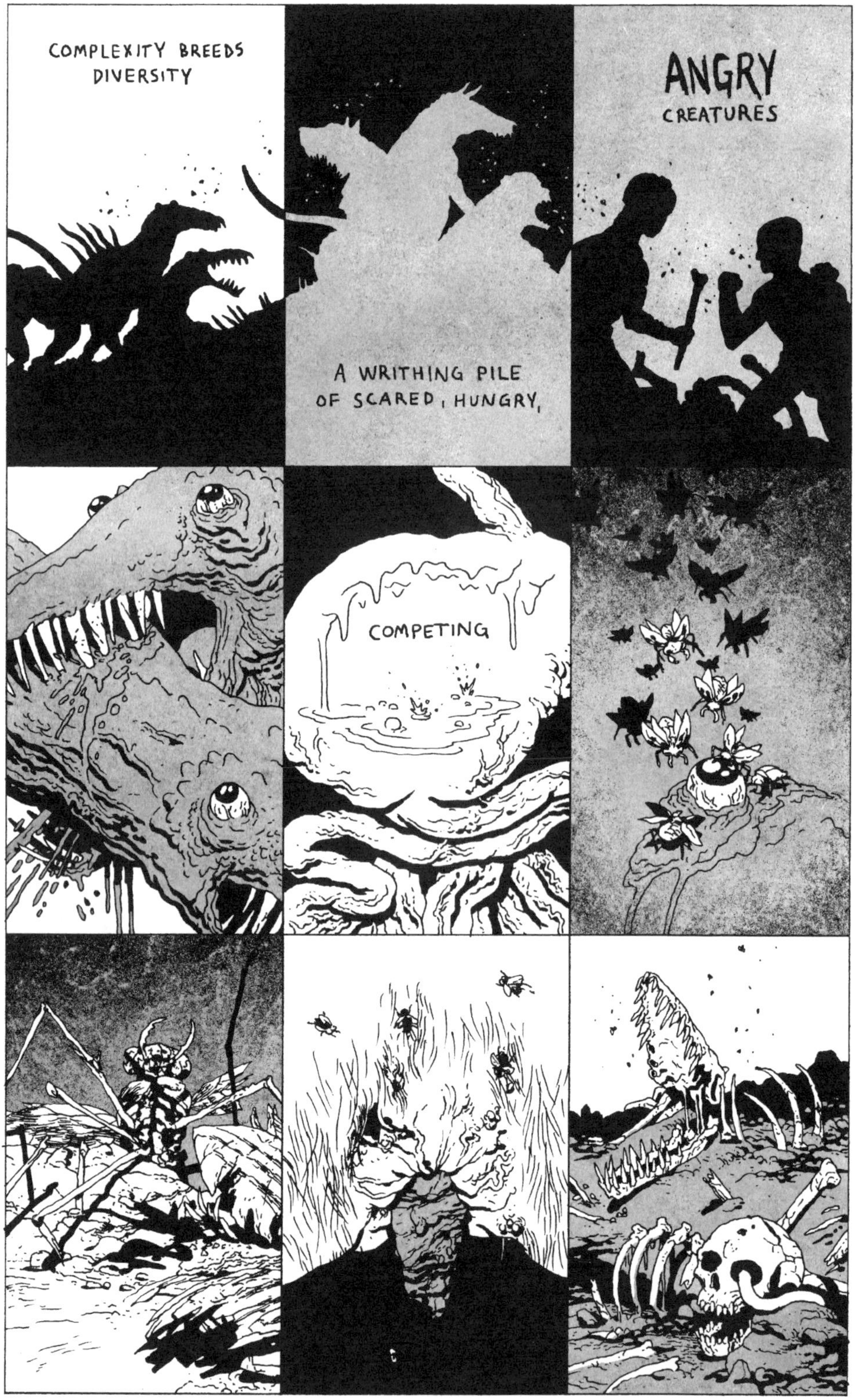
COMPLEXITY BREEDS DIVERSITY
A WRITHING PILE OF SCARED, HUNGRY,
ANGRY CREATURES
COMPETING

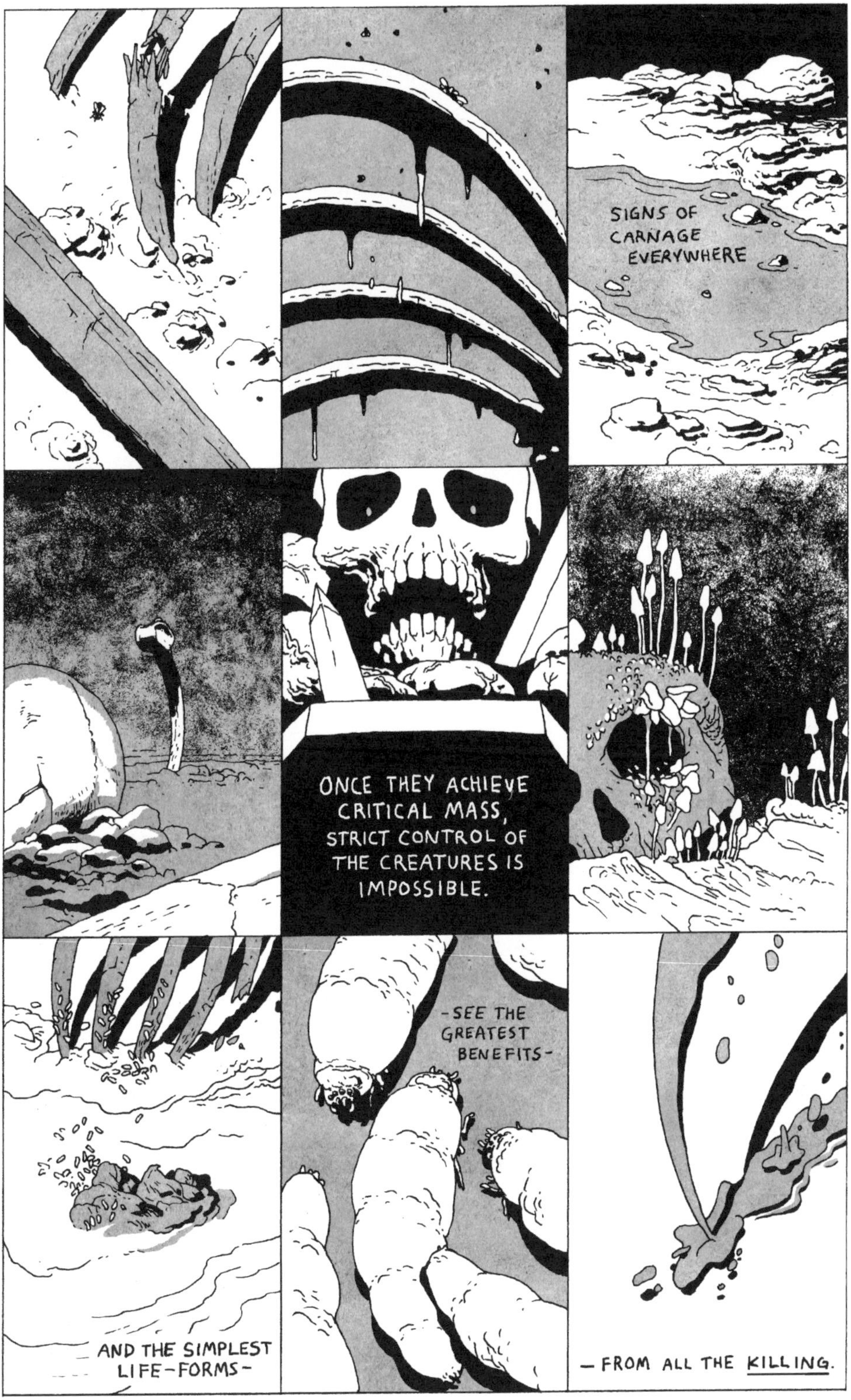
SIGNS OF CARNAGE EVERYWHERE
ONCE THEY ACHIEVE CRITICAL MASS, STRICT CONTROL OF THE CREATURES IS IMPOSSIBLE.
AND THE SIMPLEST LIFE-FORMS-
-SEE THE GREATEST BENEFITS-
- FROM ALL THE KILLING.

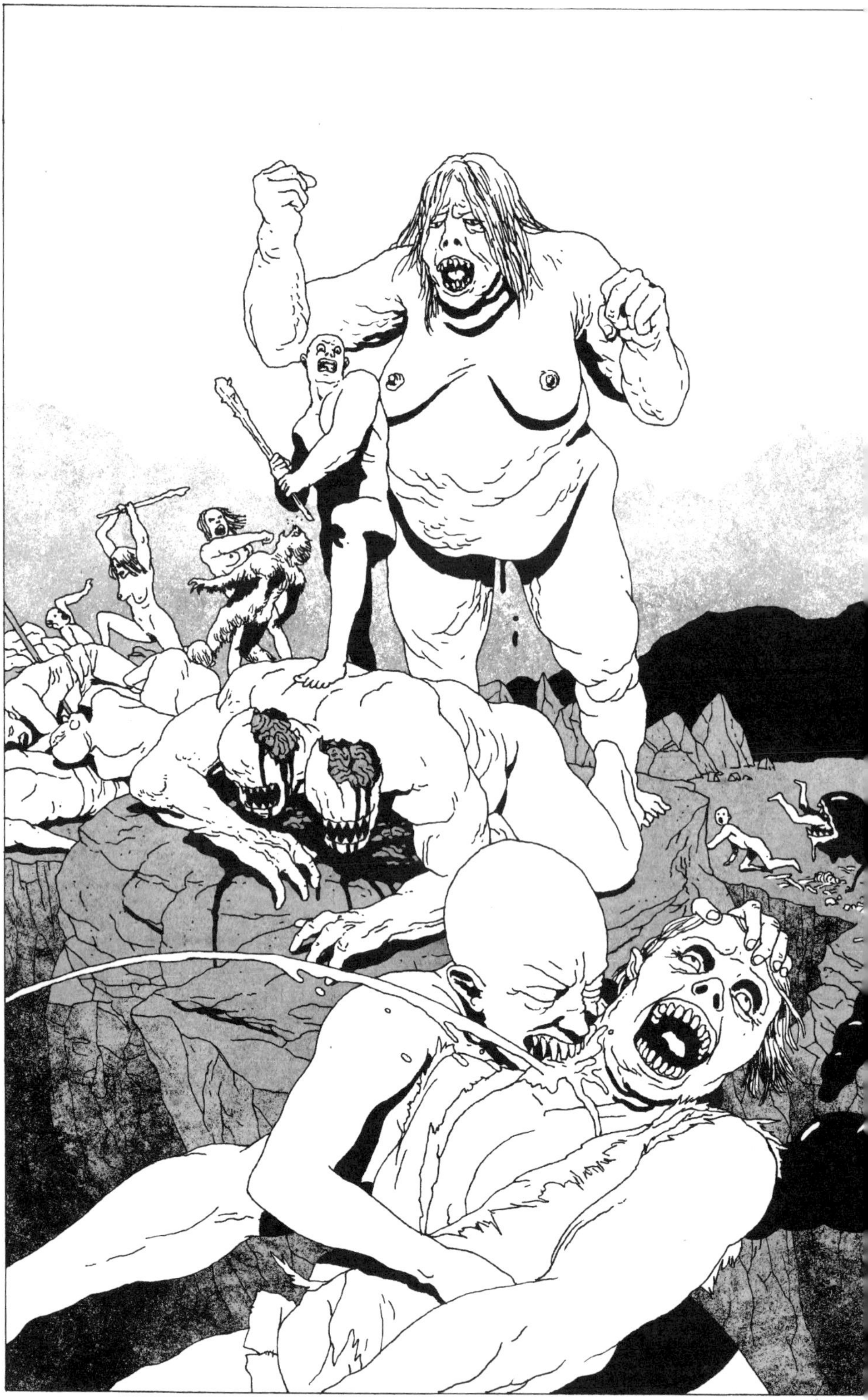

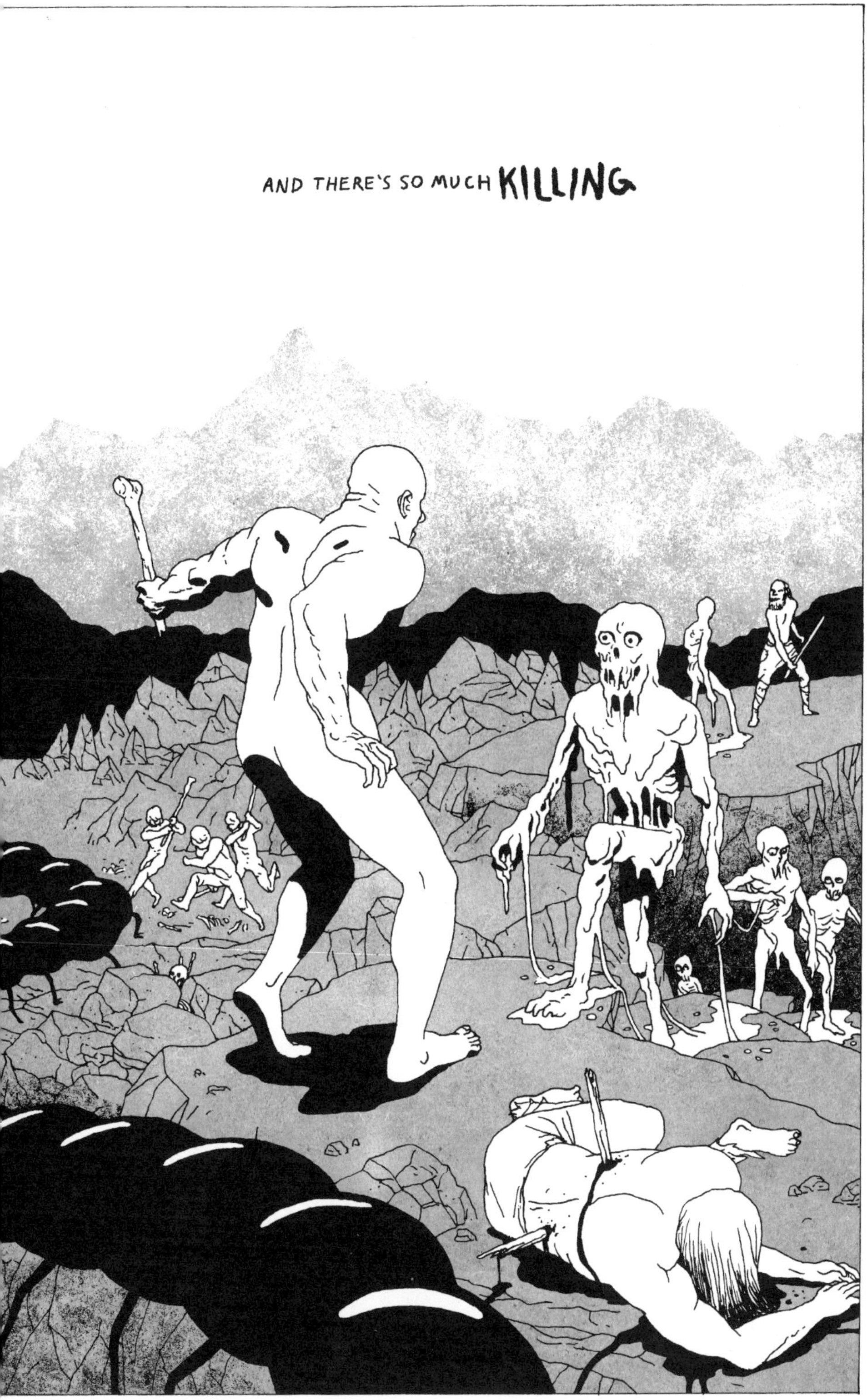
AND THERE'S SO MUCH KILLING

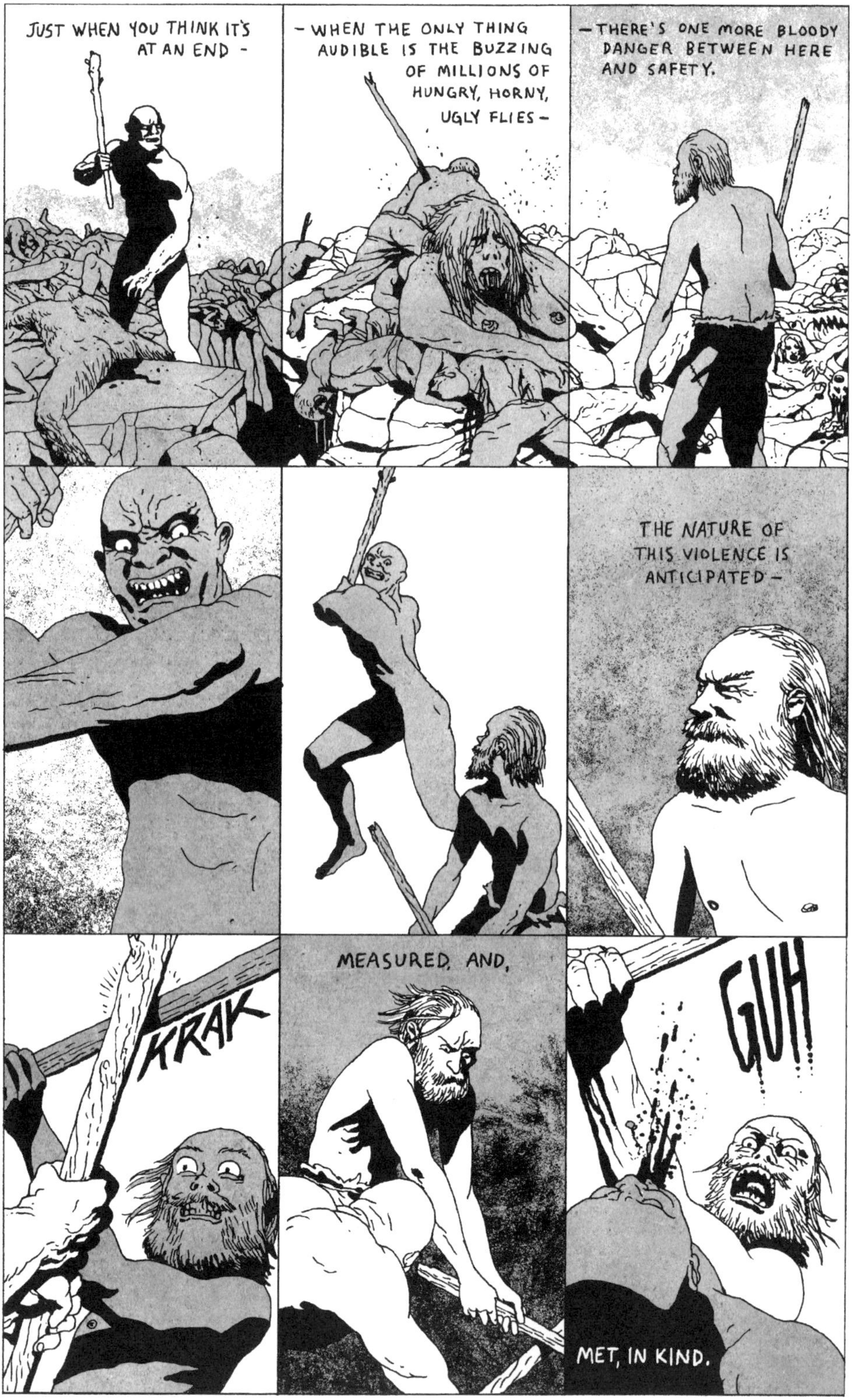
JUST WHEN YOU THINK IT'S AT AN END -
- WHEN THE ONLY THING AUDIBLE IS THE BUZZING OF MILLIONS OF HUNGRY, HORNY, UGLY FLIES -
- THERE'S ONE MORE BLOODY DANGER BETWEEN HERE AND SAFETY.
THE NATURE OF THIS VIOLENCE IS ANTICIPATED -
KRAK
MEASURED, AND,
GUH
MET, IN KIND.

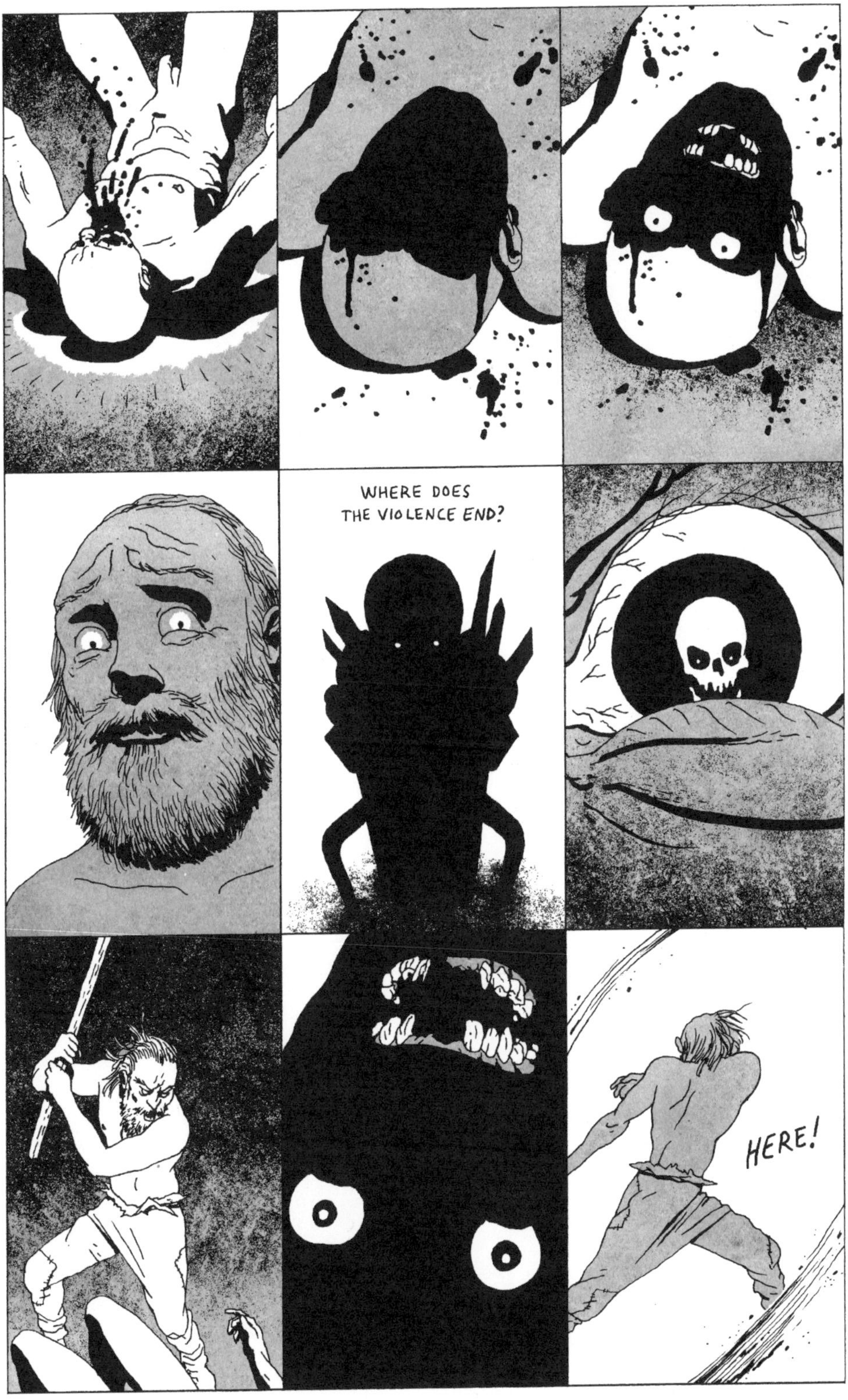
WHERE DOES
THE VIOLENCE END?
HERE!

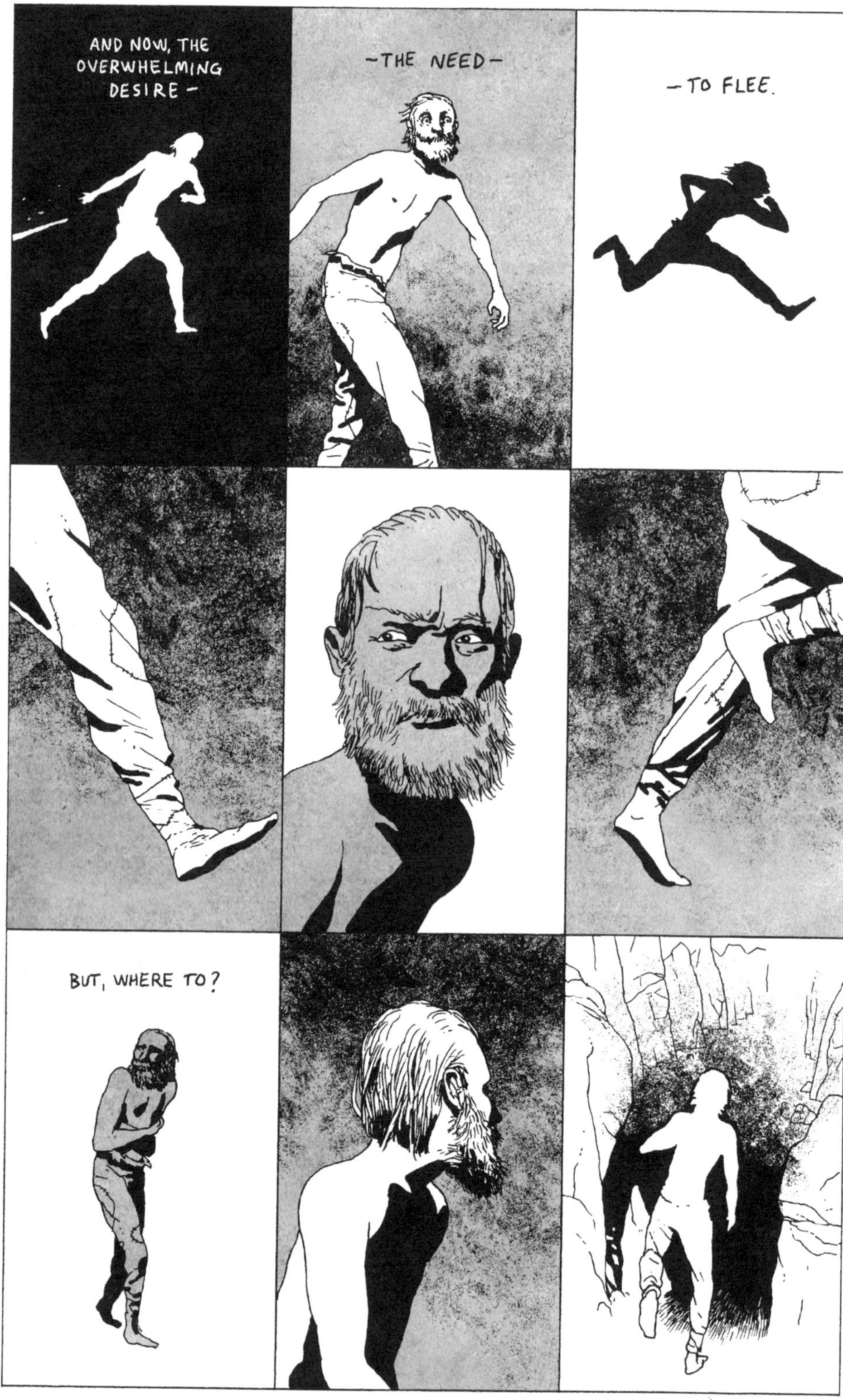
AND NOW, THE OVERWHELMING DESIRE -
-THE NEED-
-TO FLEE.
BUT, WHERE TO?

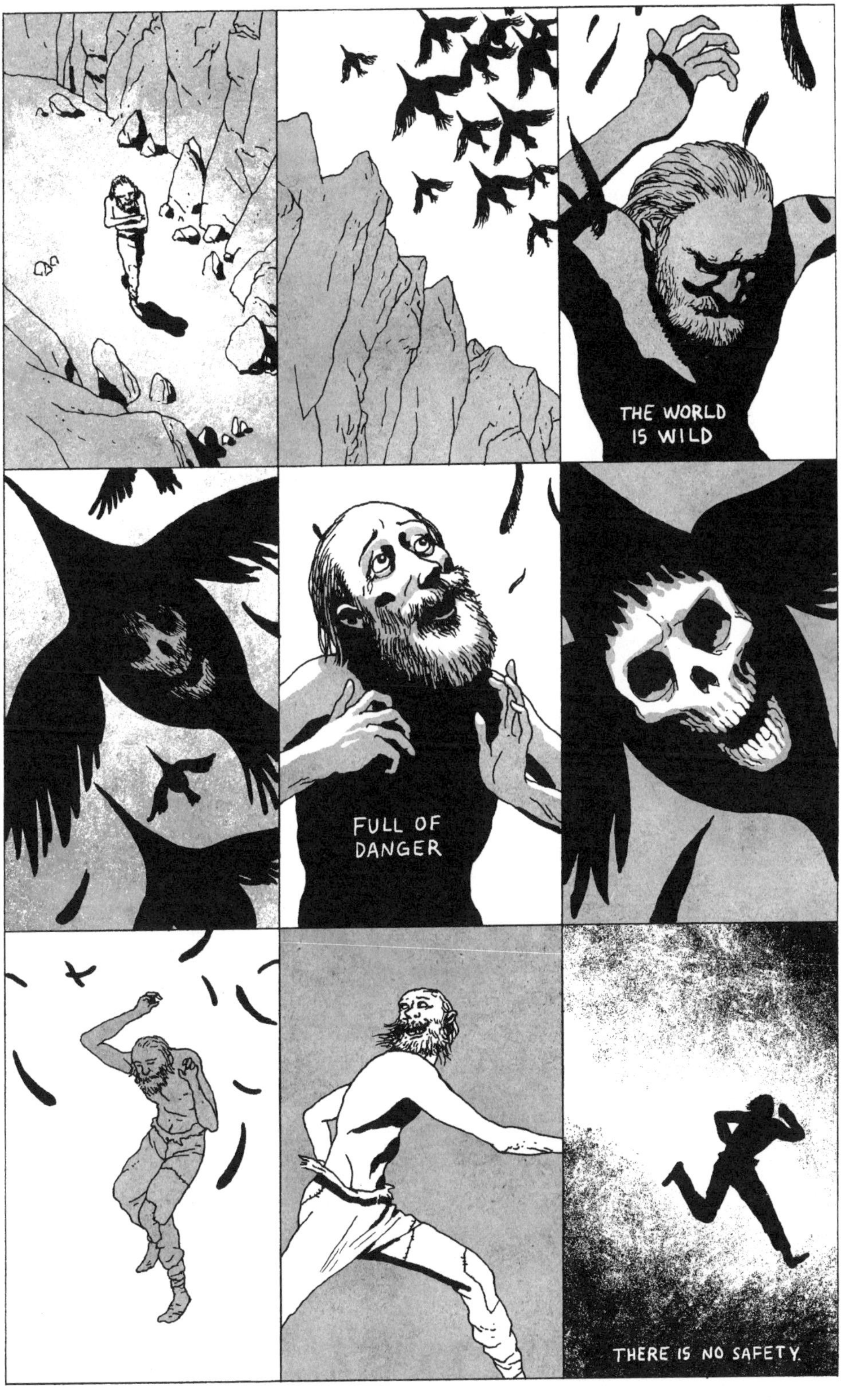
THE WORLD IS WILD
FULL OF DANGER
THERE IS NO SAFETY.

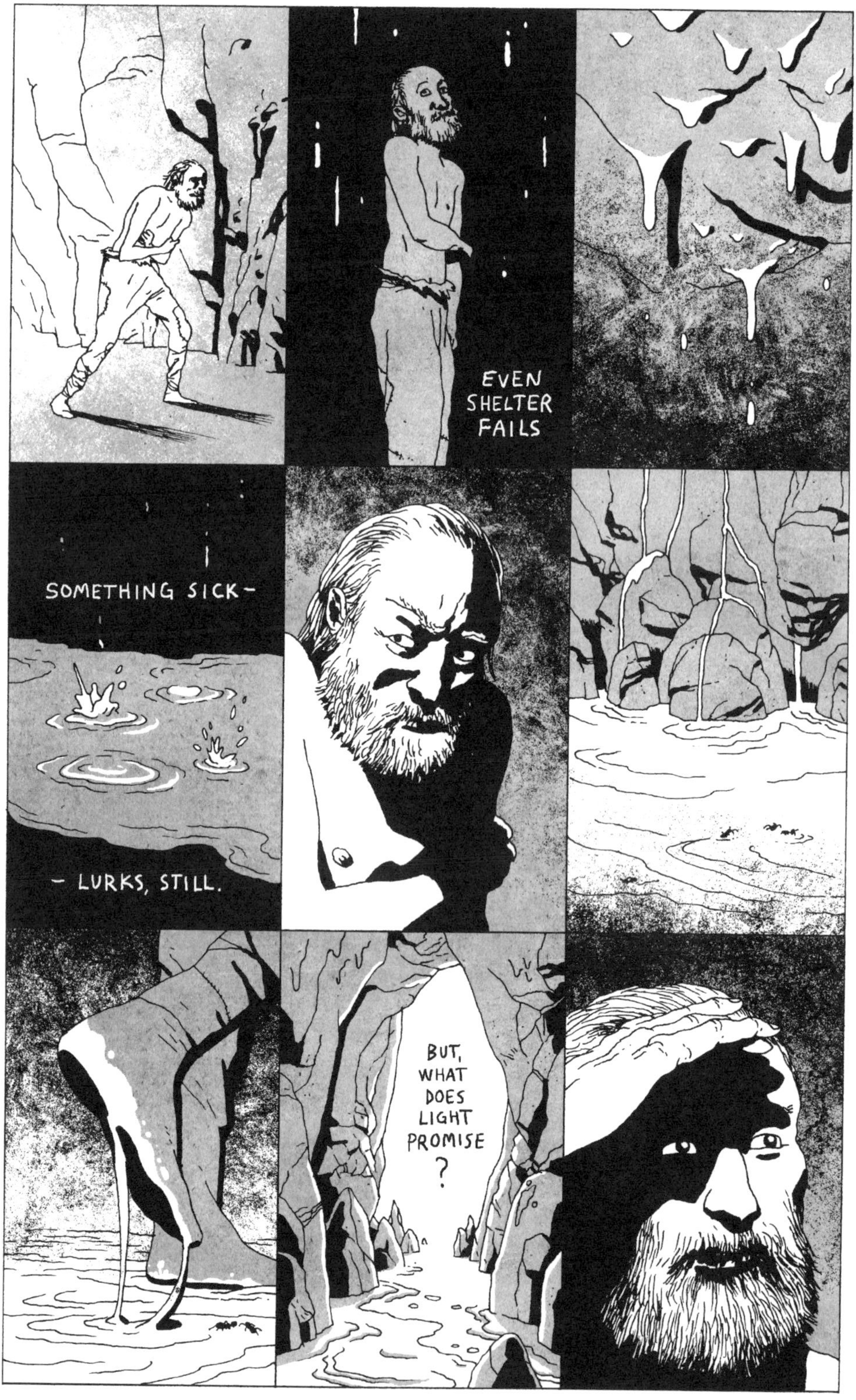
EVEN SHELTER FAILS
SOMETHING SICK-
- LURKS, STILL.
BUT, WHAT DOES LIGHT PROMISE ?

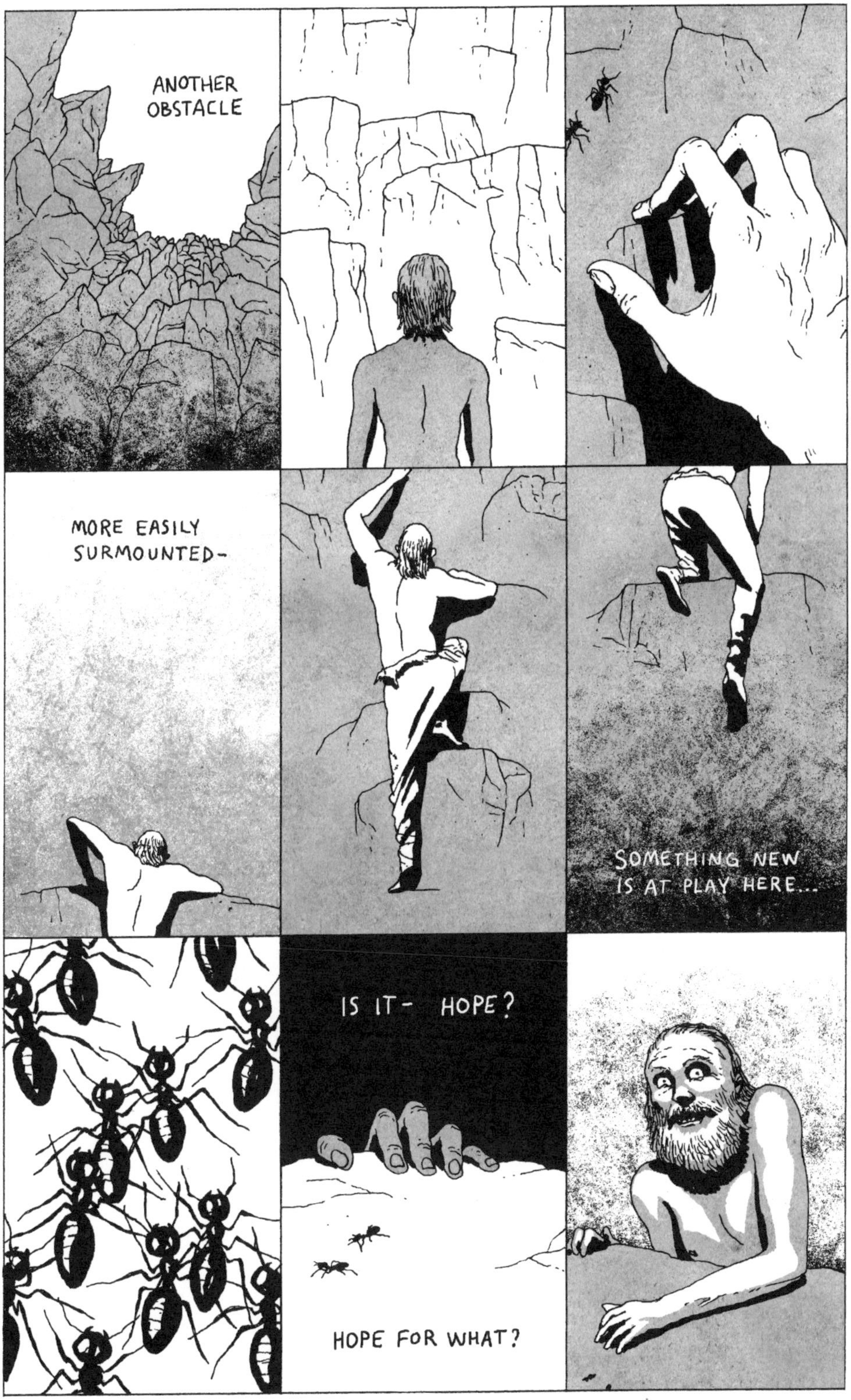
ANOTHER OBSTACLE
MORE EASILY SURMOUNTED-
SOMETHING NEW IS AT PLAY HERE...
IS IT- HOPE?
HOPE FOR WHAT?

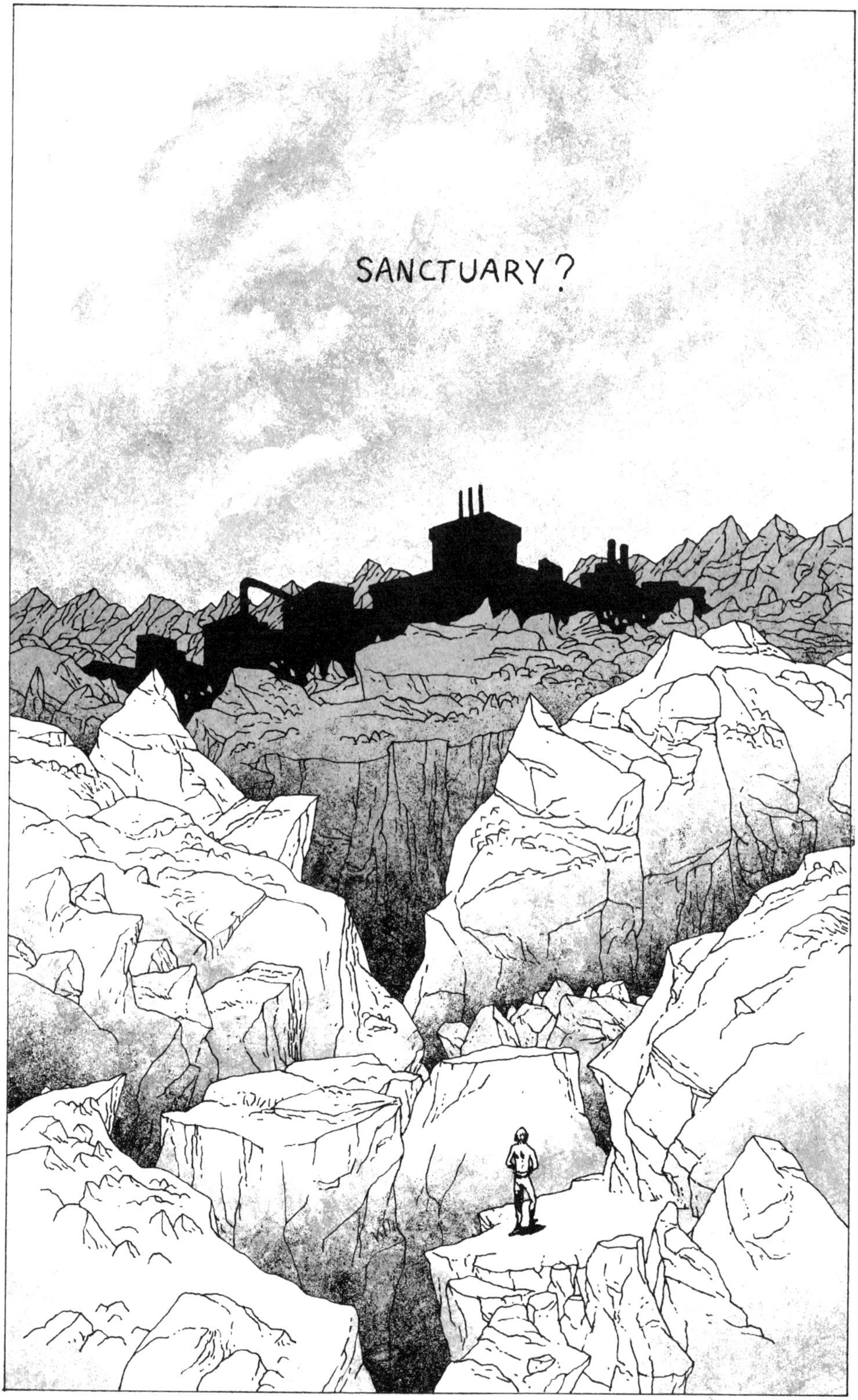
SANCTUARY?

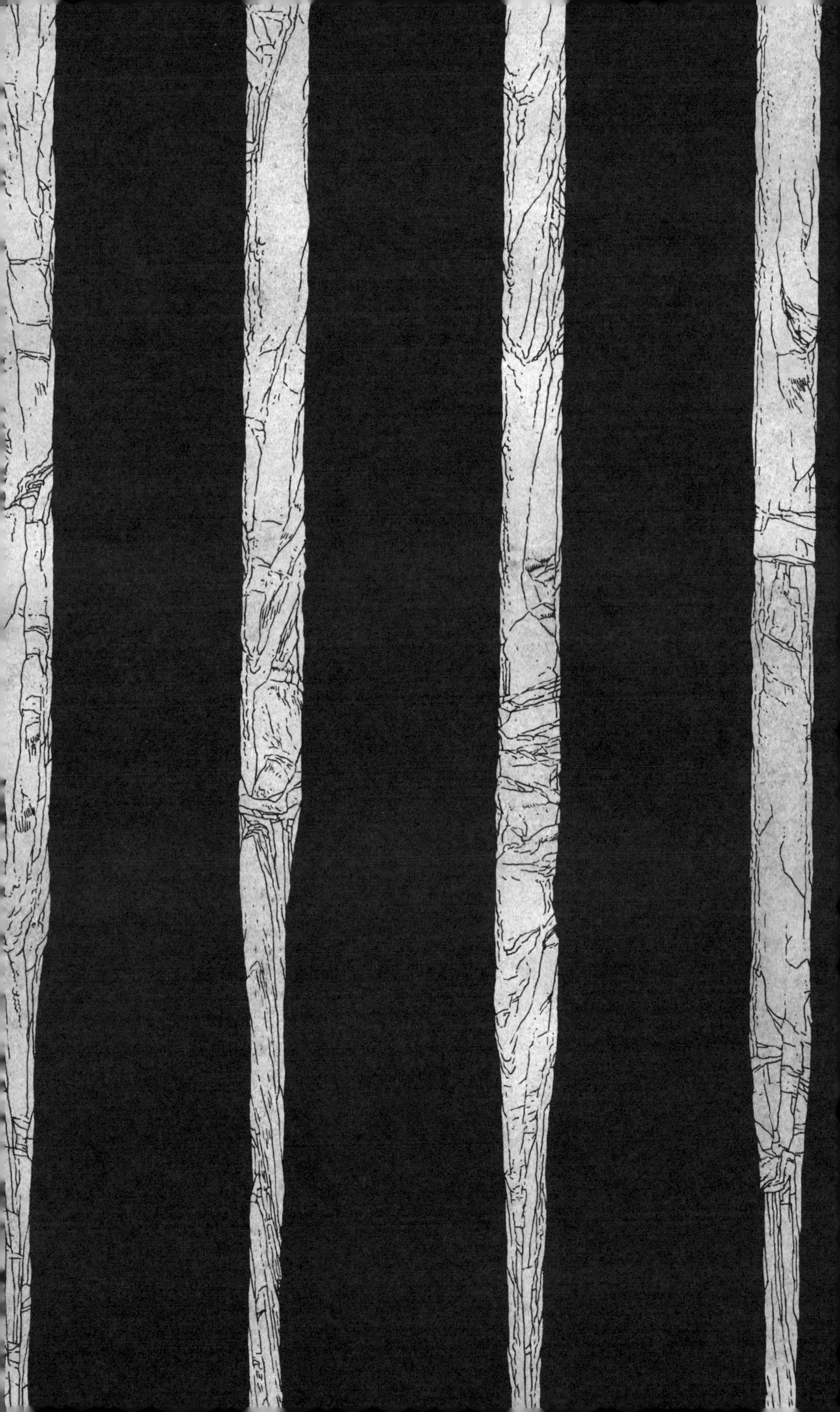

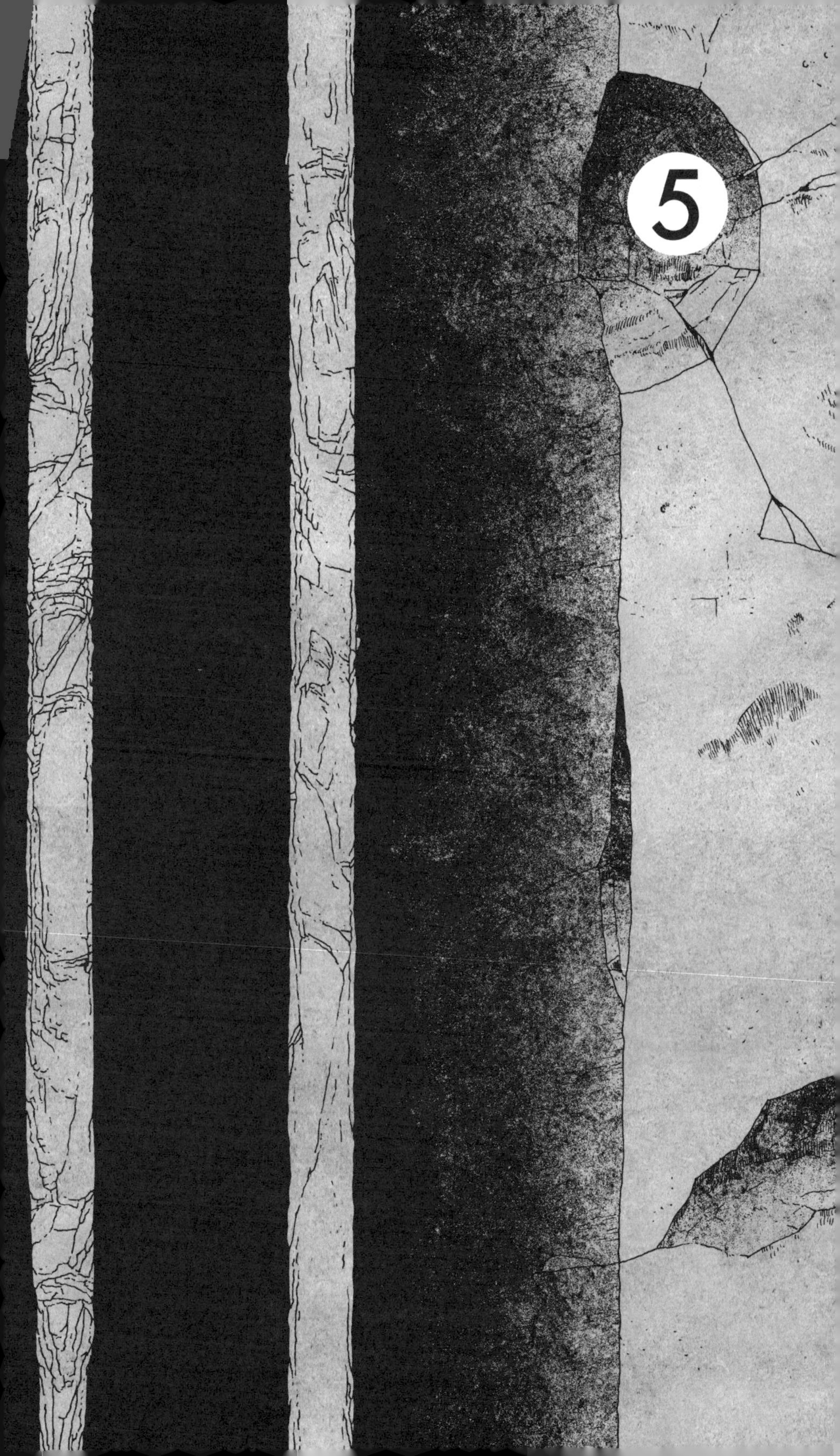
5

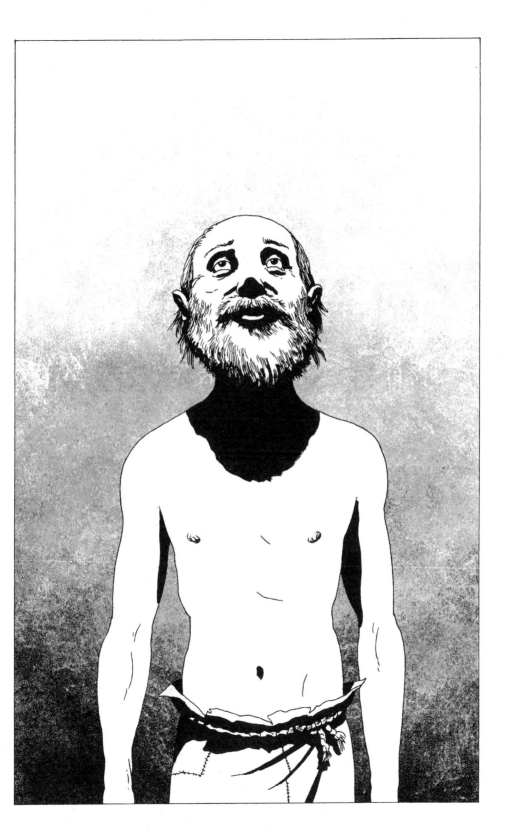

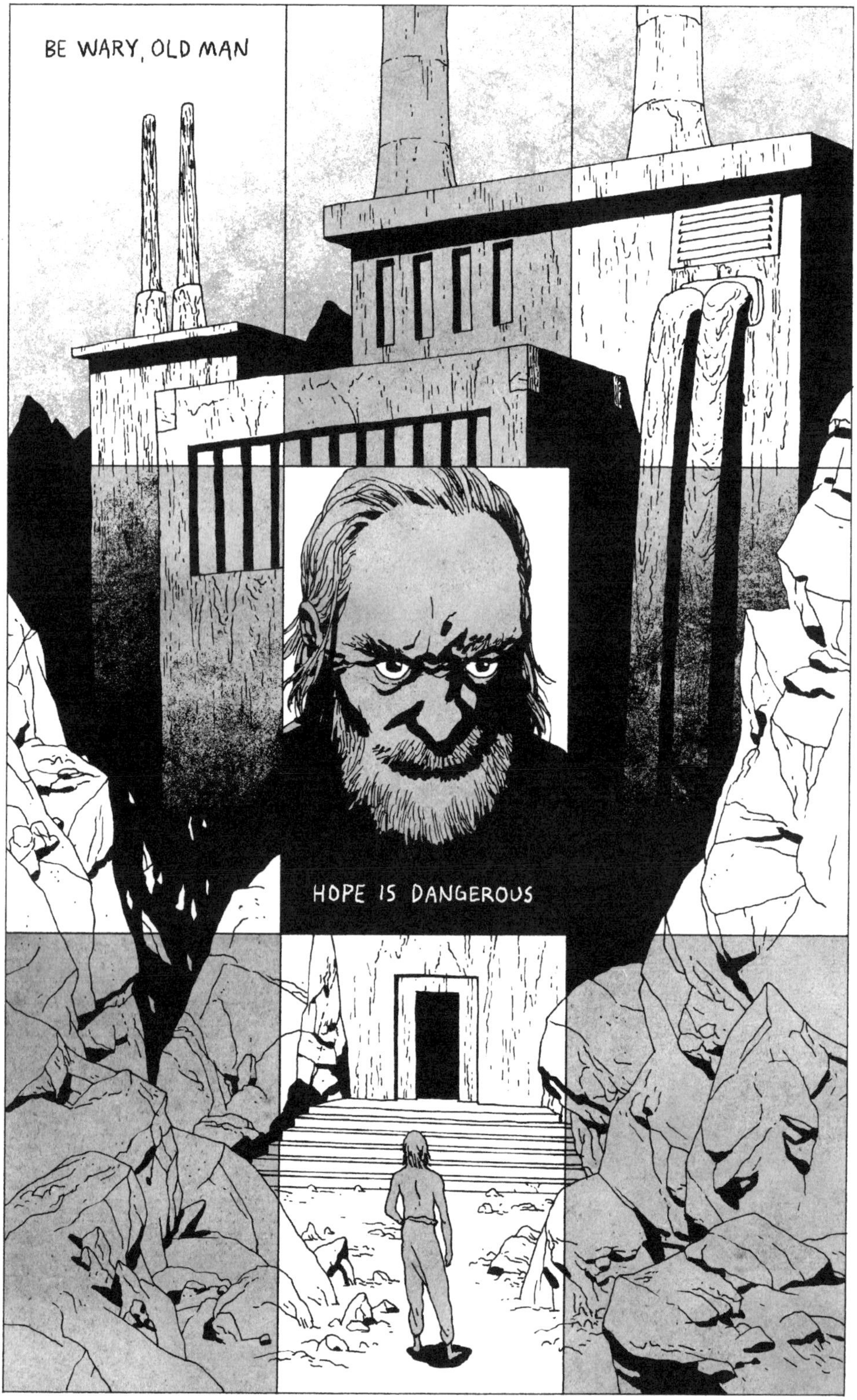
BE WARY, OLD MAN
HOPE IS DANGEROUS

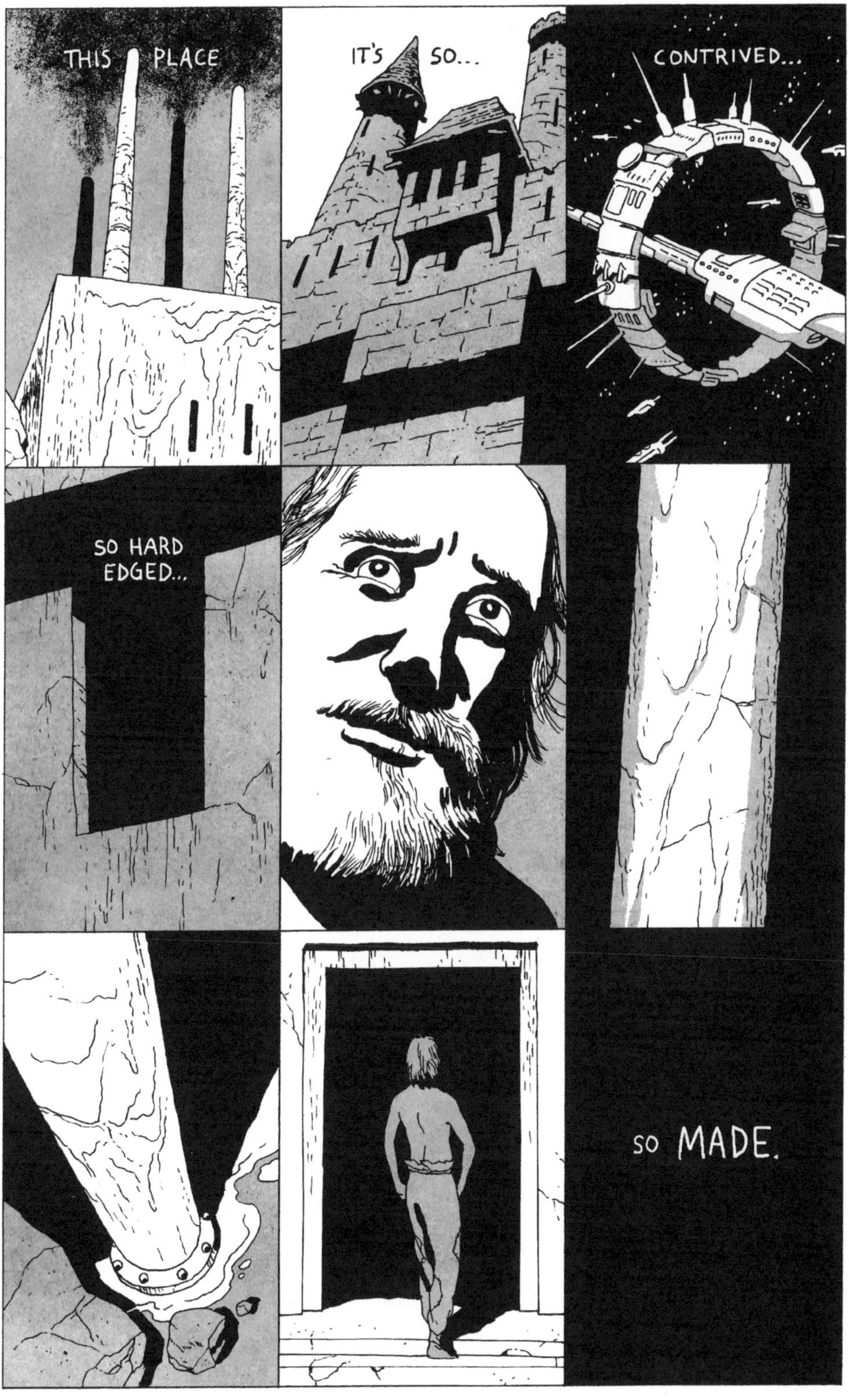
THIS PLACE
IT'S SO...
CONTRIVED...
SO HARD EDGED...
SO MADE.

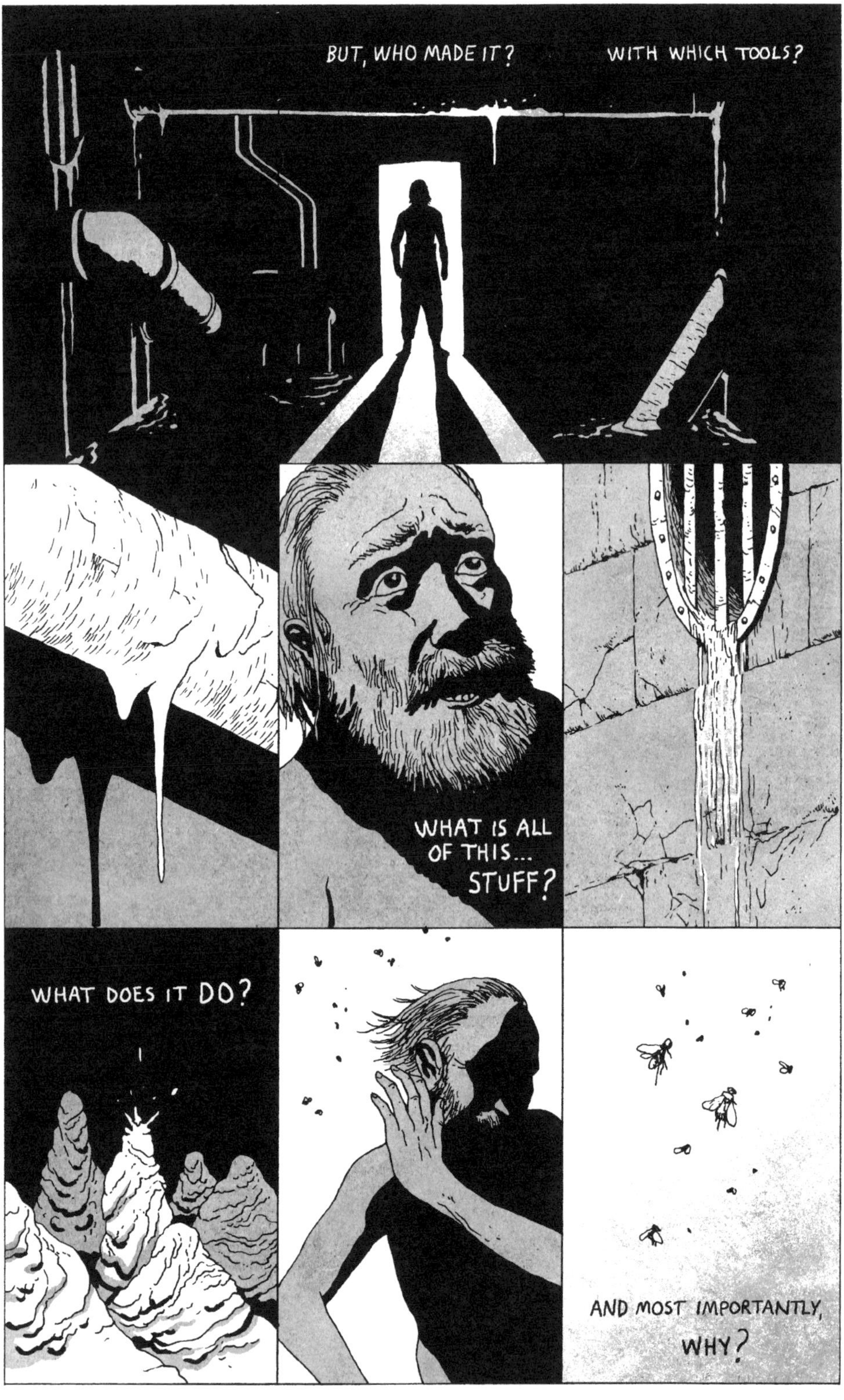
BUT, WHO MADE IT?
WITH WHICH TOOLS?
WHAT IS ALL OF THIS... STUFF?
WHAT DOES IT DO?
AND MOST IMPORTANTLY, WHY?

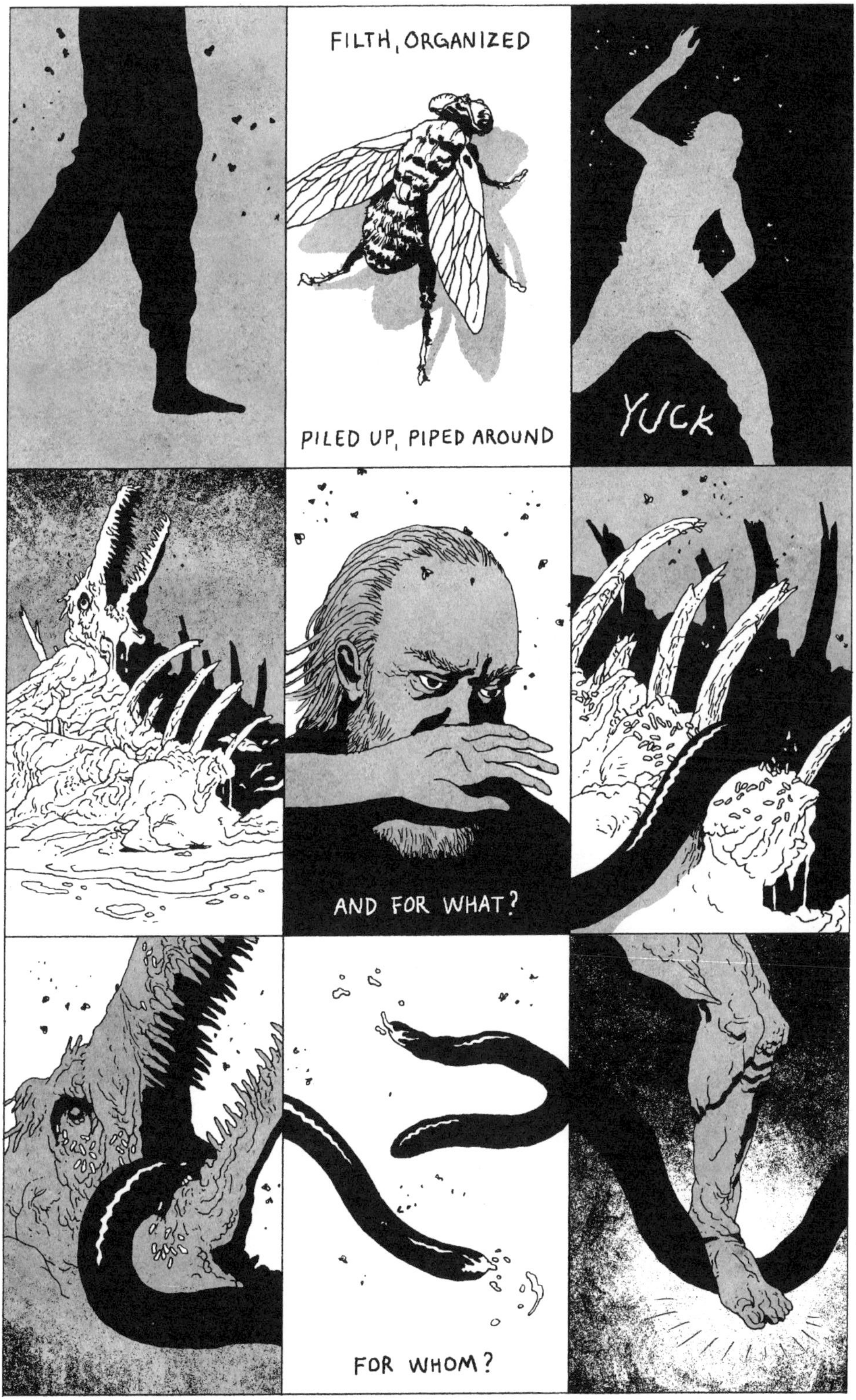
FILTH, ORGANIZED
PILED UP, PIPED AROUND
YUCK
AND FOR WHAT?
FOR WHOM?

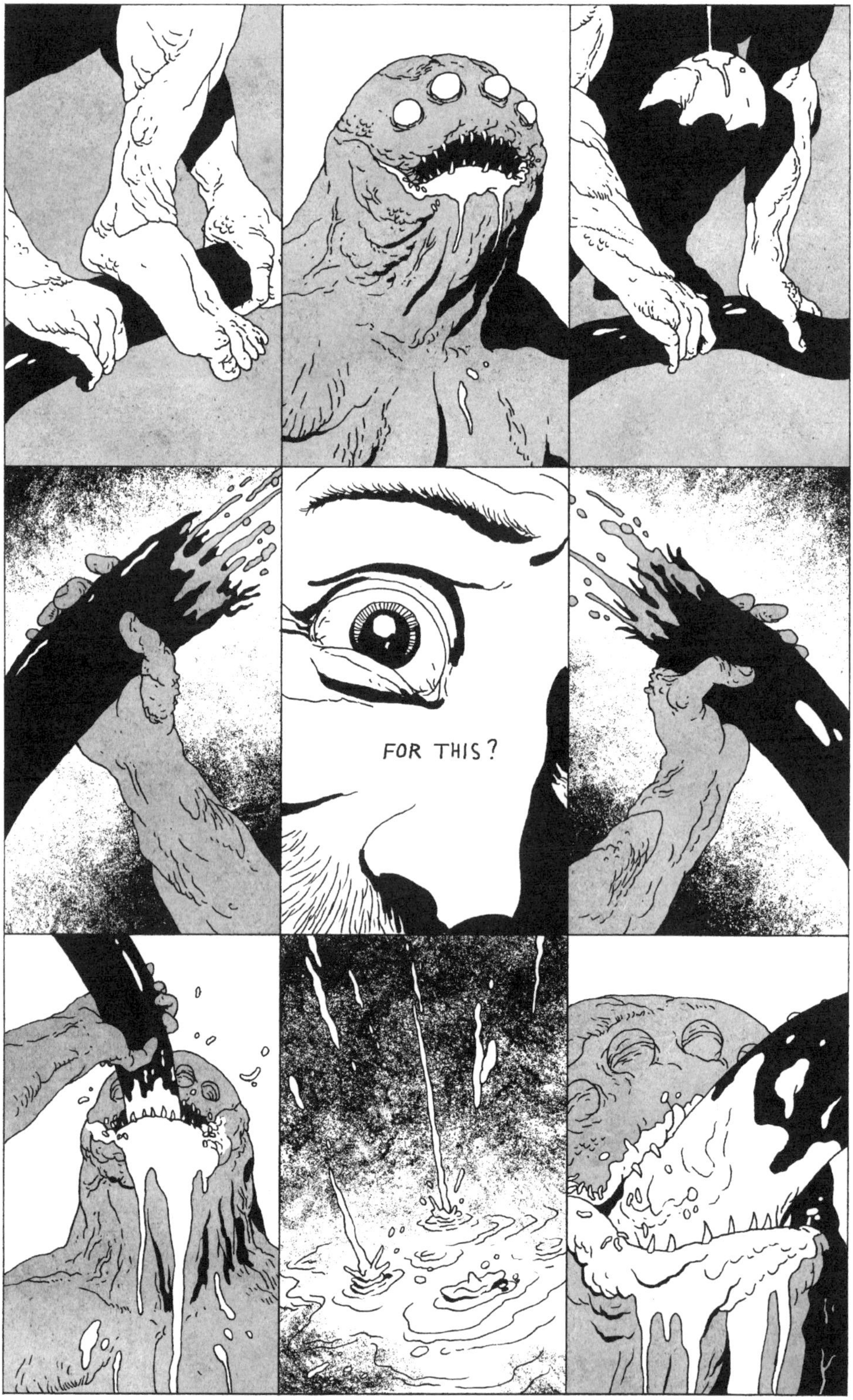
FOR THIS?

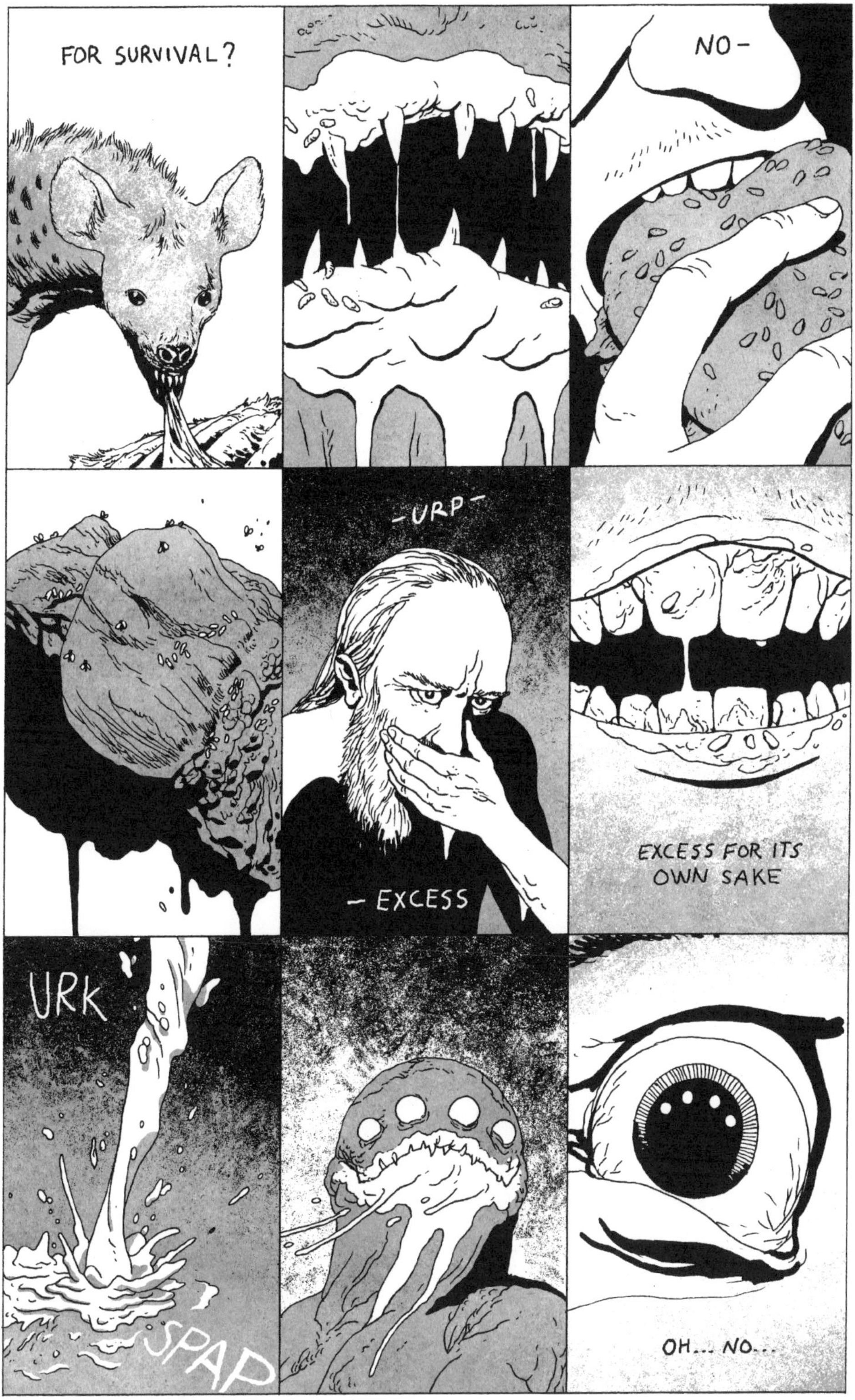
FOR SURVIVAL?
NO-
-URP-
- EXCESS
EXCESS FOR ITS OWN SAKE
URK
SPAP
OH... NO...

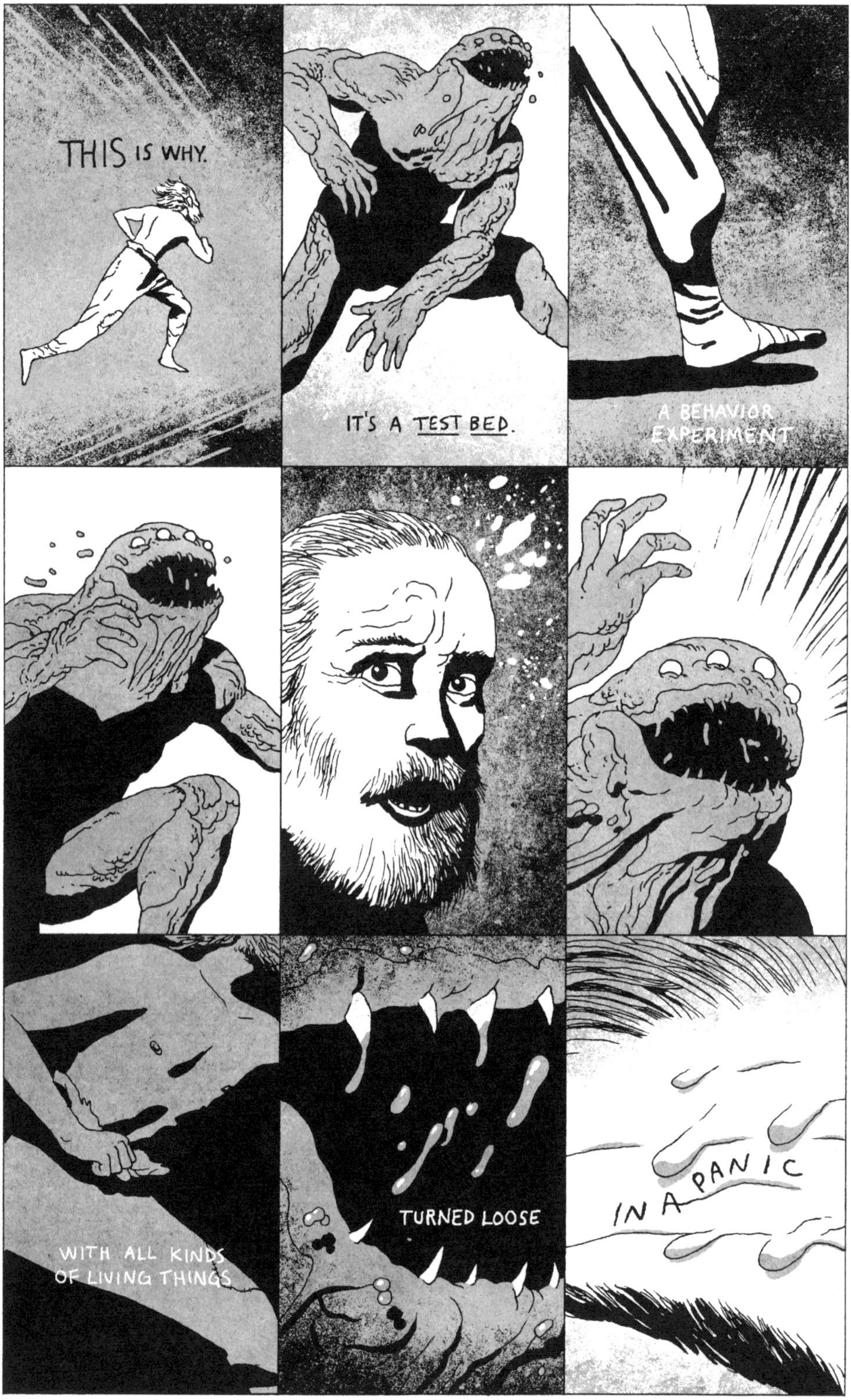
THIS IS WHY.
IT'S A TEST BED.
A BEHAVIOR EXPERIMENT
WITH ALL KINDS OF LIVING THINGS
TURNED LOOSE
IN A PANIC

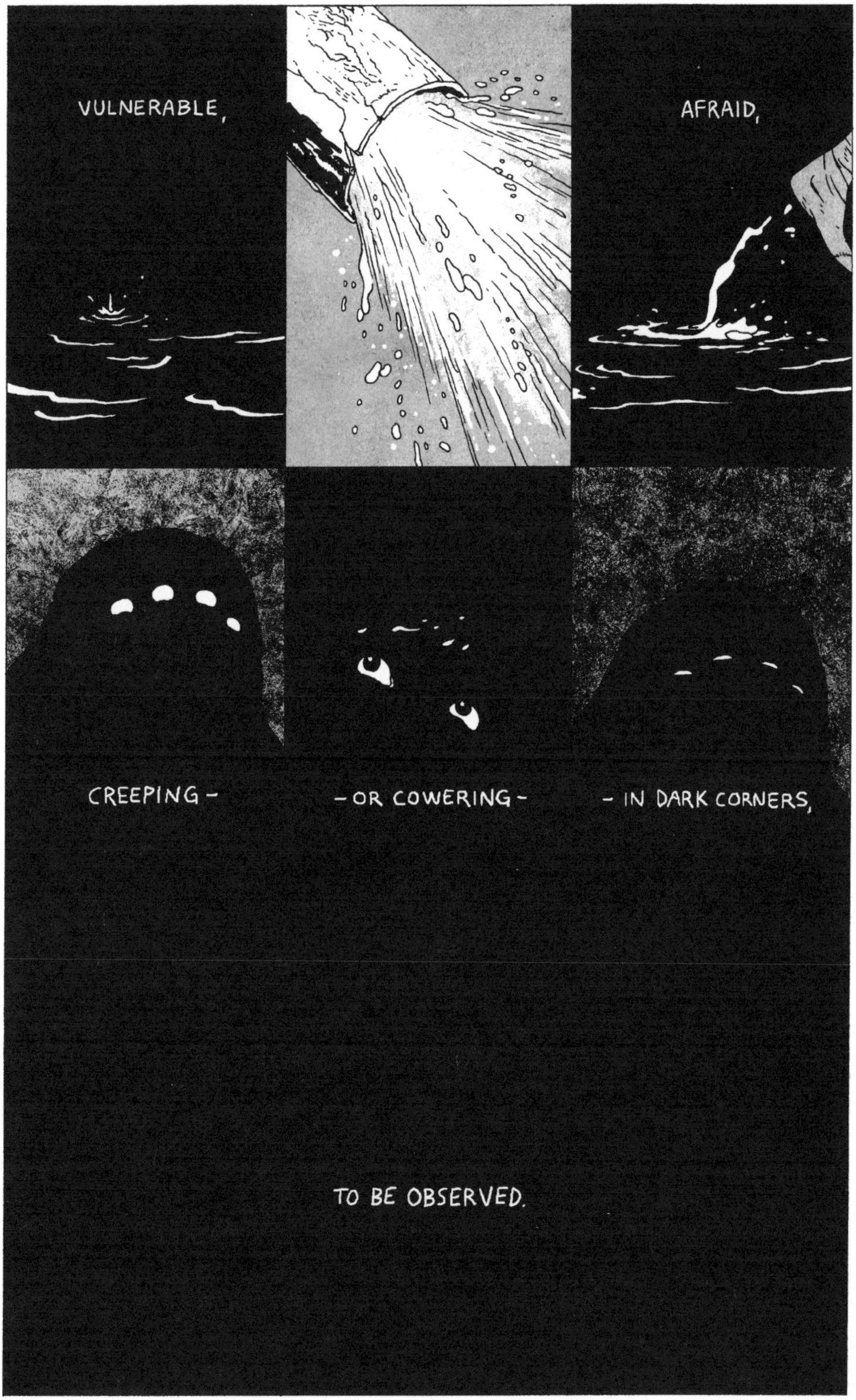
VULNERABLE,
AFRAID,
CREEPING -
- OR COWERING -
- IN DARK CORNERS,
TO BE OBSERVED.

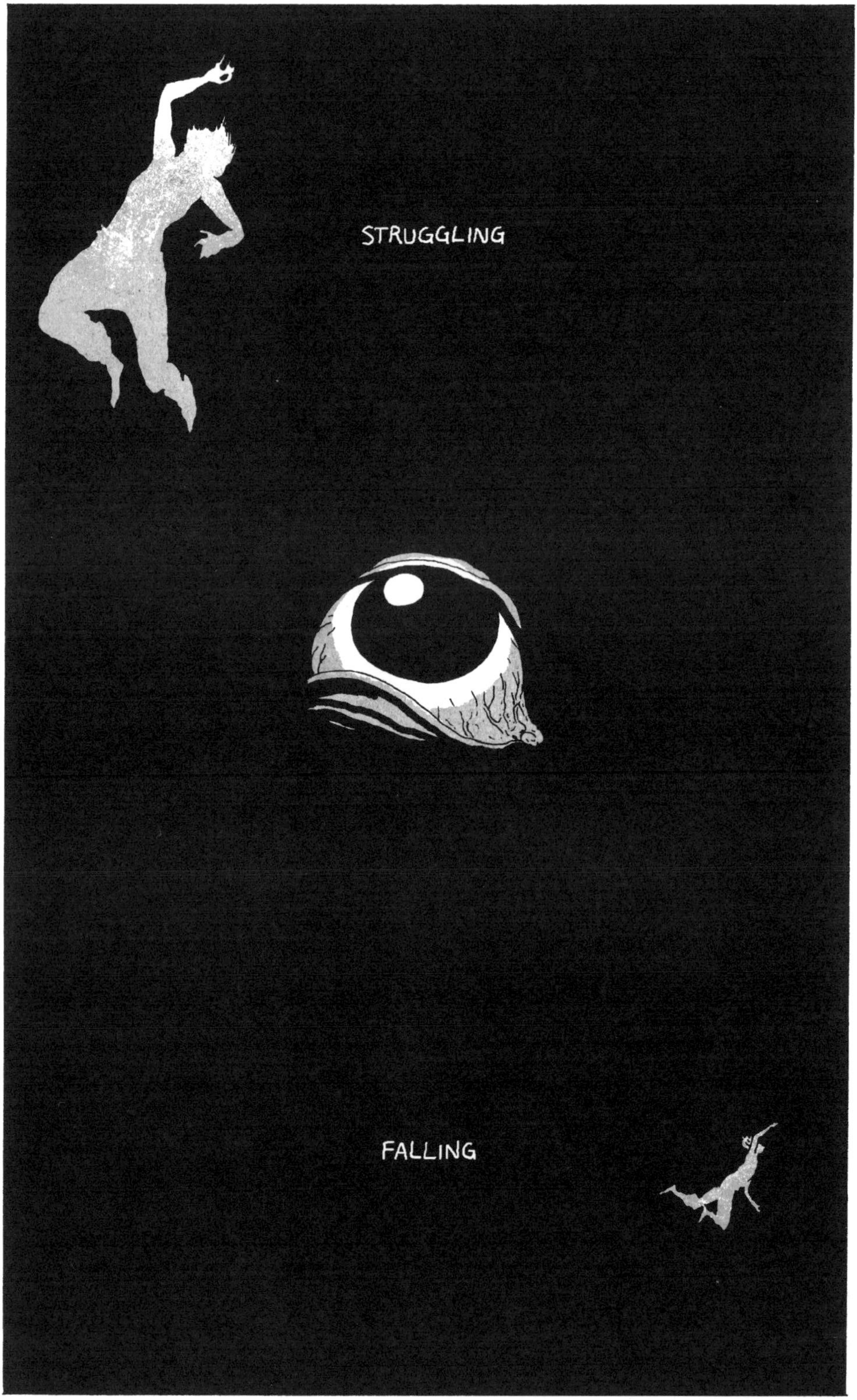
STRUGGLING
FALLING

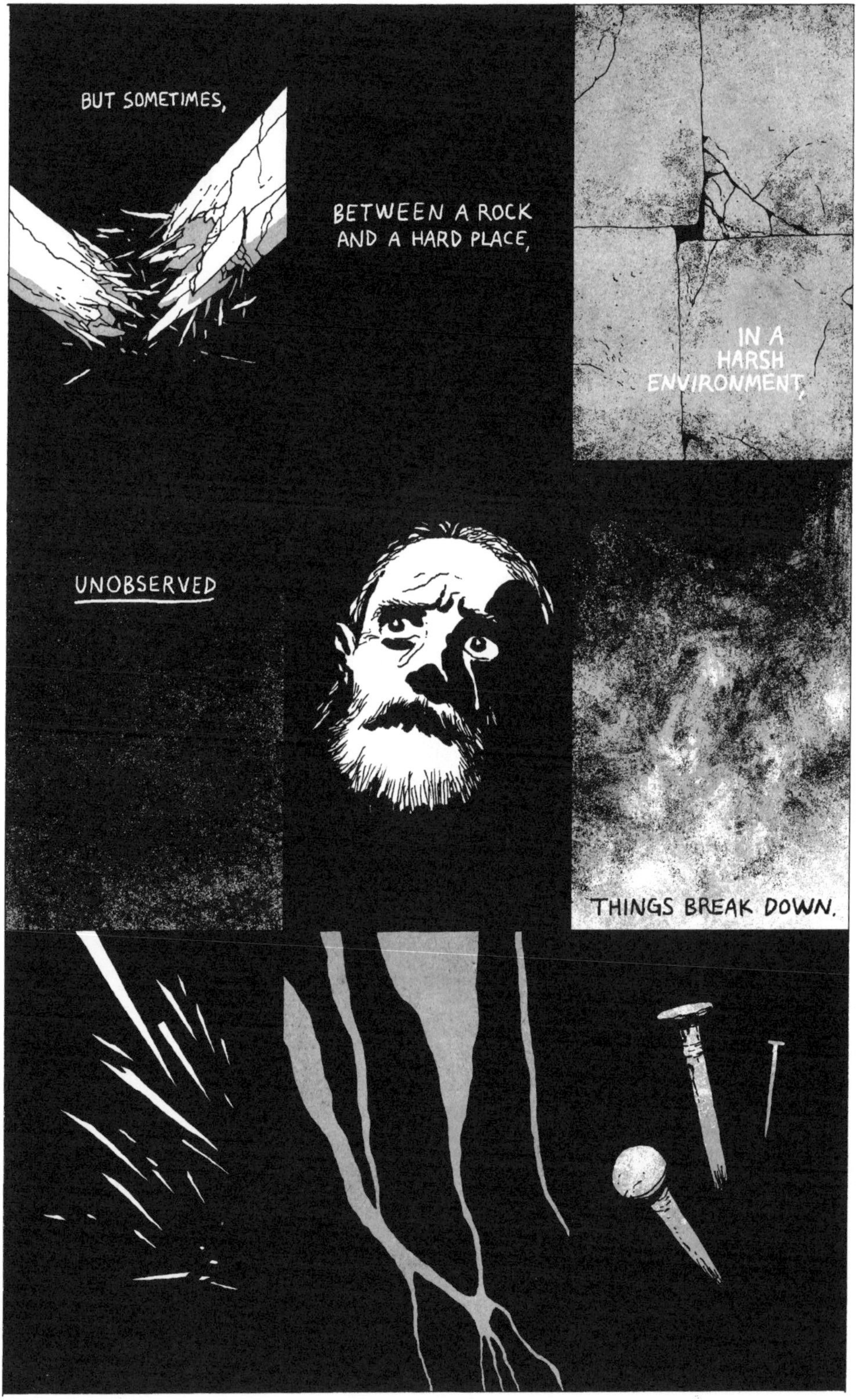
BUT SOMETIMES,
BETWEEN A ROCK AND A HARD PLACE,
IN A HARSH ENVIRONMENT,
UNOBSERVED
THINGS BREAK DOWN.

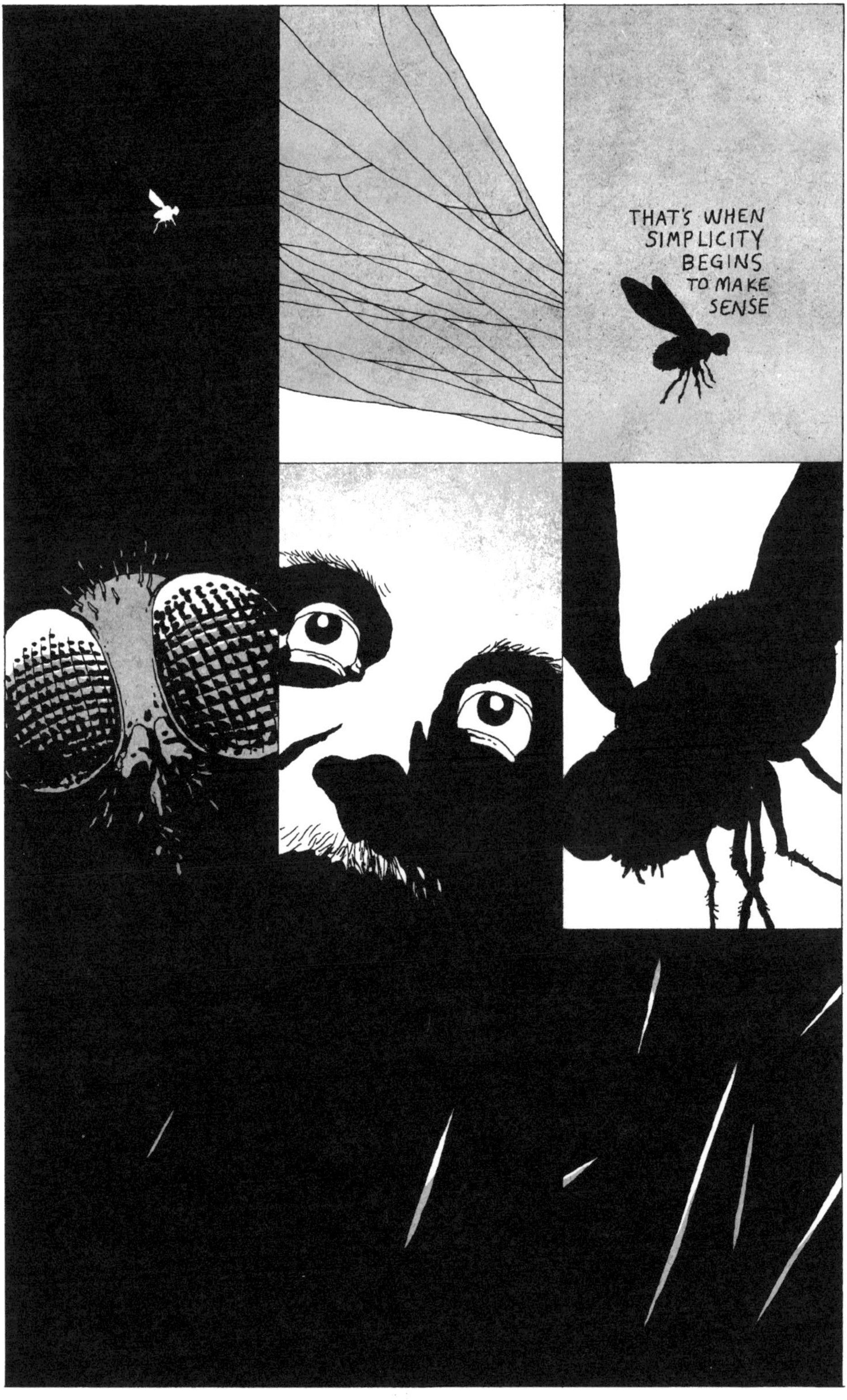
THAT'S WHEN SIMPLICITY BEGINS TO MAKE SENSE

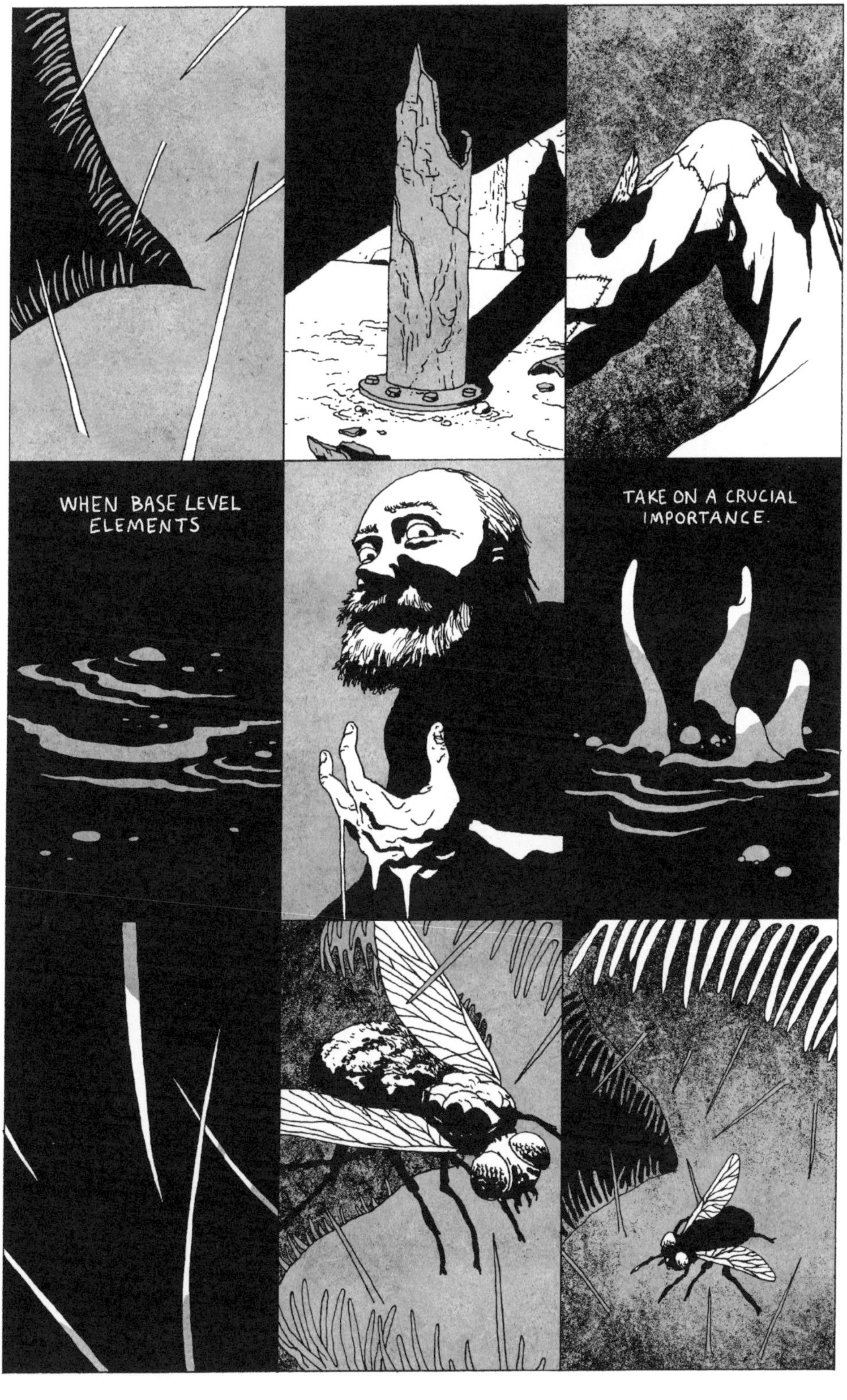
WHEN BASE LEVEL ELEMENTS
TAKE ON A CRUCIAL IMPORTANCE.

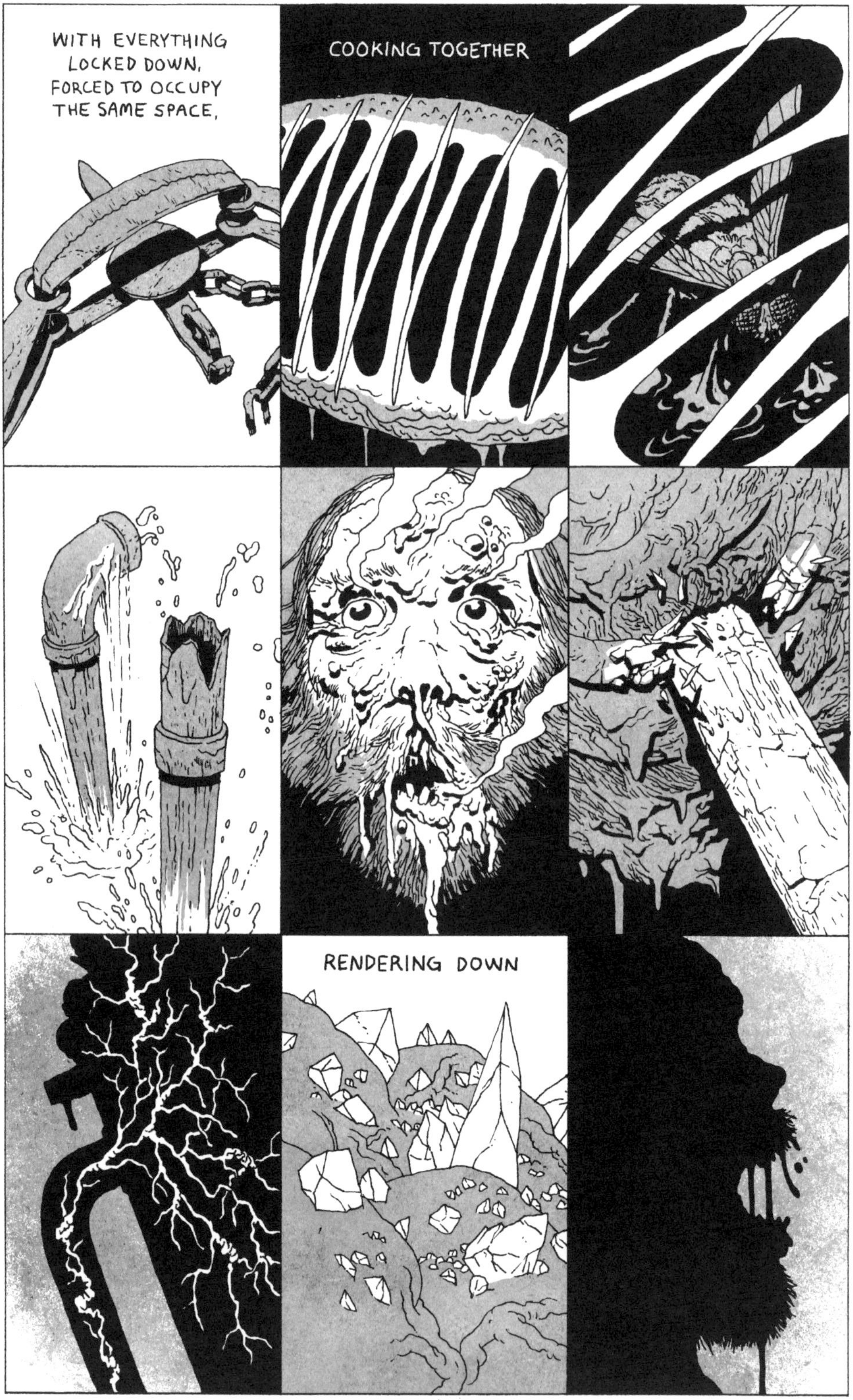
WITH EVERYTHING LOCKED DOWN, FORCED TO OCCUPY THE SAME SPACE,
COOKING TOGETHER
RENDERING DOWN

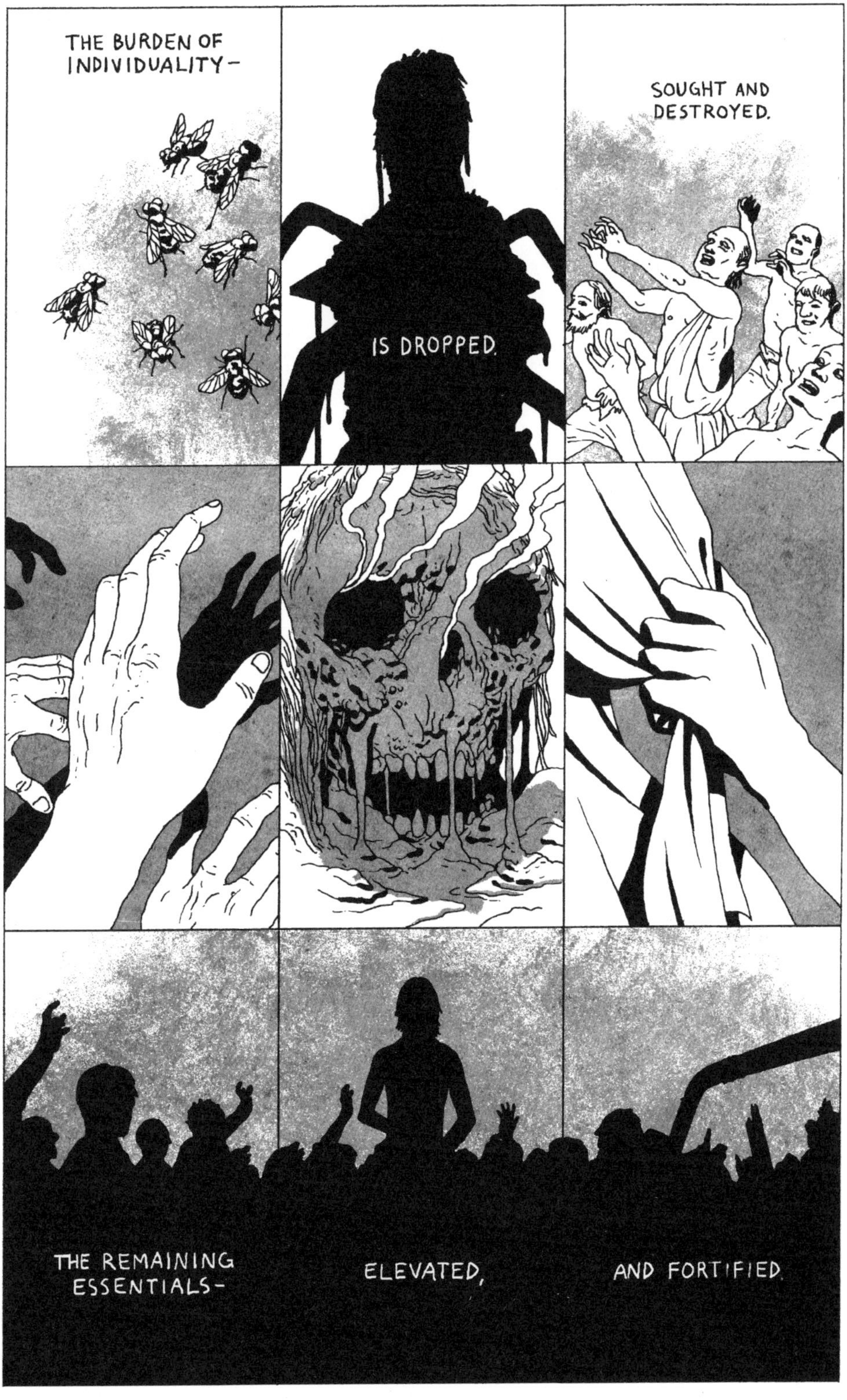
THE BURDEN OF INDIVIDUALITY-
IS DROPPED.
SOUGHT AND DESTROYED.
THE REMAINING ESSENTIALS-
ELEVATED,
AND FORTIFIED.

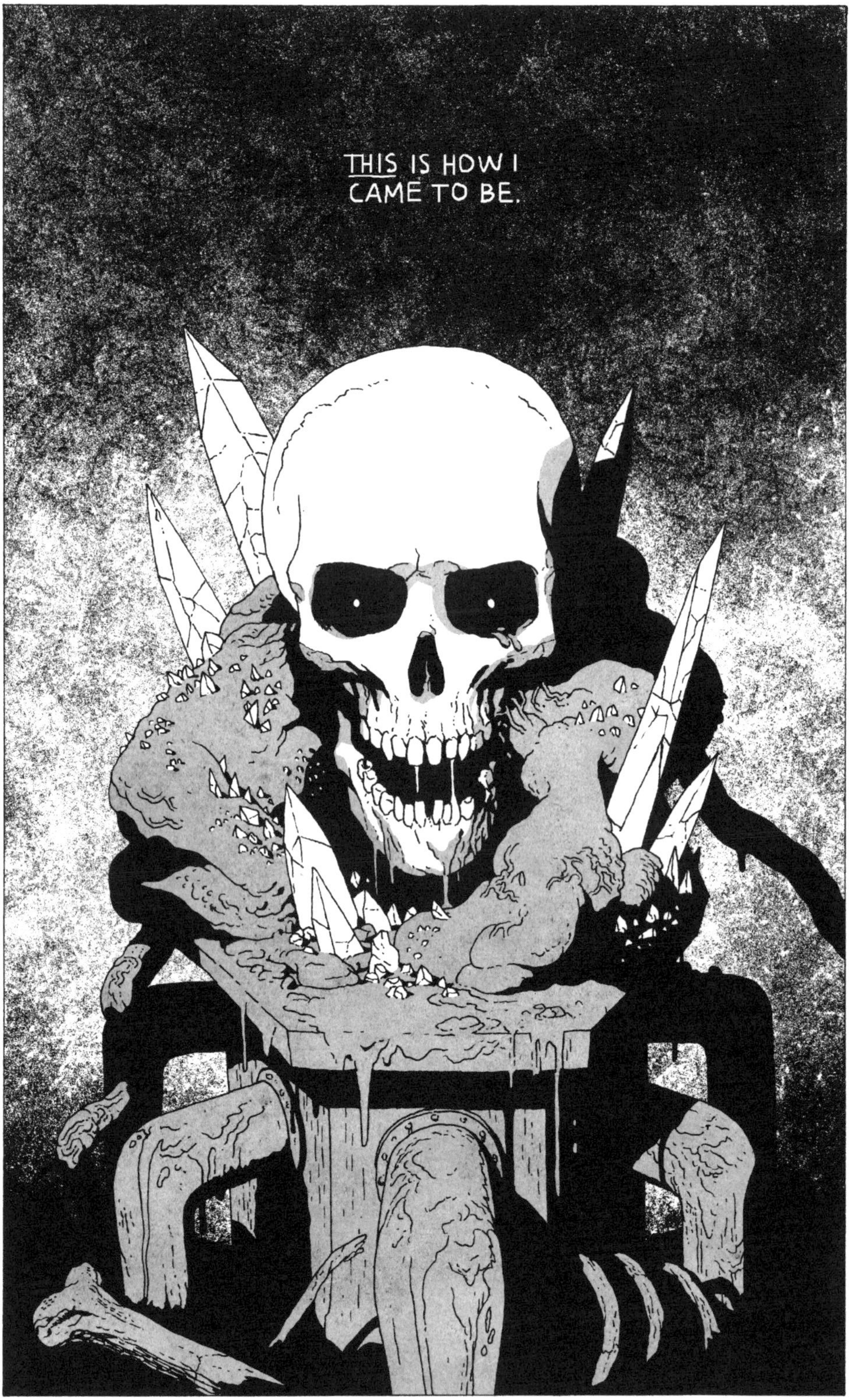
THIS IS HOW I
CAME TO BE.

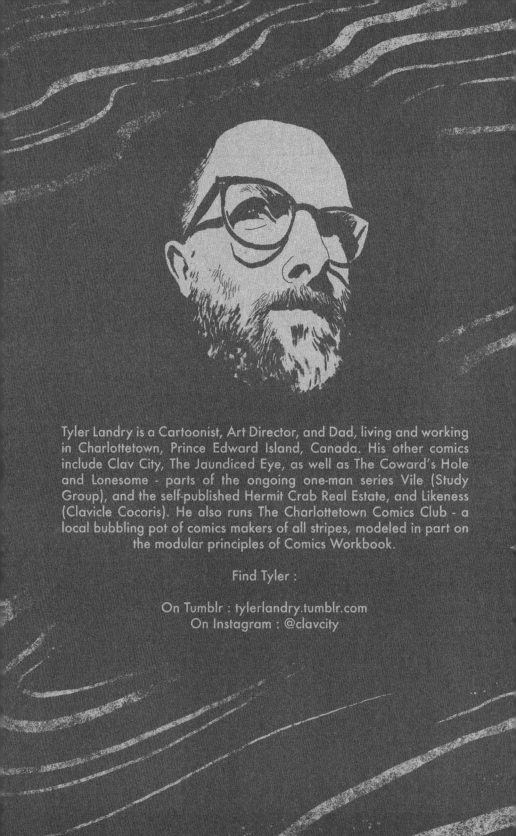

Tyler Landry is a Cartoonist, Art Director, and Dad, living and working in Charlottetown, Prince Edward Island, Canada. His other comics include Clav City, The Jaundiced Eye, as well as The Coward's Hole and Lonesome - parts of the ongoing one-man series Vile (Study Group), and the self-published Hermit Crab Real Estate, and Likeness (Clavicle Cocoris). He also runs The Charlottetown Comics Club - a local bubbling pot of comics makers of all stripes, modeled in part on the modular principles of Comics Workbook.

Find Tyler :

On Tumblr : tylerlandry.tumblr.com
On Instagram : @clavcity